P9-APB-919

THE
JEWISH
BIBLE
almanac

THE JEWISH BIBLE almanac

RONALD H. ISAACS

JASON ARONSON INC.
Northvale, New Jersey
Jerusalem

This book was set in 12 pt. Times Roman by Alabama Book Composition of Deatsville, Alabama.

Library of Congress Cataloging-in-Publication Data

Isaacs, Ronald H.
    The Jewish Bible almanac / by Ronald H. Isaacs.
        p.   cm.
    Includes bibliographical references and index.
    ISBN 0-7657-9961-8 (alk. paper)
    1. Bible. O.T.—Dictionaries. I. Title.
BS440.I83   1997
221.3—dc21   97-11324

Manufactured in the United States of America. Jason Aronson Inc. offers books and cassettes. For information and catalog write to Jason Aronson Inc., 230 Livingston Street, Northvale, NJ 07647.

The heavens belong to God
but the earth God gave to humans
PSALM 115:16

Contents

Preface

The Bible is the oldest and most widely read book in our civilization. It has been in continuous circulation for almost 2,000 years and has been the source of religious ideals and values for countless millions of people. Ever since Sinai, the moral imperatives of The Five Books of Moses and the books of the Prophets have provided great inspiration to social reformers and religious idealists.

Throughout the English-speaking world many famous novelists, poets, and dramatists have studied the Bible for its profound ideas, rich language, and original style. Political ideas and institutions of American life have been shaped by the teachings of the Bible.

It is in the realm of religion that the Bible is of paramount importance. Since it is the holy book of both Judaism and Christianity, its influence has been significant within the whole ethical framework of Western civilization.

The Bible has been the Magna Carta of the impoverished and oppressed. Historically, no country has had a constitution in which the interests of the people are so highly upheld as they are in the Bible. It has been said that the Bible is the most democratic book in the world. And undoubtedly, people throughout the ages have always recognized it as a great spiritual heritage for all of humankind.

This volume presents a unique collection of curious facts and oddities, unusual statistics, and Bible information in a list form that vividly brings to life the Bible and its people. The alphabetical arrangement is intended to help the reader locate the material in a quick and user-friendly manner. It is my hope that the book will entertain, inform, challenge, and stimulate you, thus increasing your desire to study the Bible, one of the all-time best-selling books.

Ronald H. Isaacs

Abominations to God

There is nothing more abhorrent in the Bible than someone or something that is an abomination to God. Abominations appear in the Bible some 116 times and vary widely in nature, including food prohibitions, idolatrous practices, magic, sexual offenses, and ethical wrongs. Here is a cross-section of biblical abominations to God:

1. The evil-minded person (Proverbs 11:20)

2. A false balance (Proverbs 11:1)

3. Sacrifices of the wicked (Proverbs 15:8)

4. Thoughts of the wicked (Proverbs 15:26)

5. A proud look (Proverbs 6:17)

6. A lying tongue (Proverbs 6:17)

7. Hands that shed innocent blood (Proverbs 6:17)

8. A heart that devises wicked imaginations (Proverbs 6:18)

1

9. Feet that are quick to run into mischief (Proverbs 6:18)

10. A false witness (Proverbs 6:19)

11. One who sows discord among brothers (Proverbs 6:19)

12. One who consigns his son or daughter to an augur, a soothsayer, a diviner, or a sorcerer (Deuteronomy 18:9)

13. A male who lies with a male (Leviticus 18:22)

Altars

The altar was originally the place where sacrificial slaughter was performed. By biblical times, however, the use of the term "altar" was extended to designate the place for offering all oblations. Altars were found everywhere in the ancient Near East. They were generally constructed from three kinds of material: stone, earth, and metal. Here is a summary of biblical altars:

1. Abraham's altars, built in Shechem, Hebron, and Moriah (Genesis 12:7–8; 13:18; 22:2, 9)

2. Ahab's altar (I Kings 16:32)

3. Balak's altar (Numbers 23:1)

4. David's altar (II Samuel 24:25)

5. Elijah's altar (I Kings 18:31–32)

6. Gideon's altar (Judges 6:24)

7. Isaac's altar (Genesis 26:25)

3

8. Jacob's altars built at Shechem and Bethel (Genesis 33:20; 35:1–7)

9. Jeroboam's altar (I Kings 12:32–33)

10. Joshua's altar (Joshua 8:30)

11. Manasseh's altar (II Kings 21:3)

12. Manoah's altar (Judges 13:20)

13. Moses' altar (Exodus 17:15)

14. Noah's altar (Genesis 8:20)

15. Samuel's altar (I Samuel 7:15, 17)

16. Saul's altar (I Samuel 14:35)

17. Uriah's altar (II Kings 16:11)

18. Zerubbabel's altar (Ezra 3:2)

America Founded on Biblical Precepts

Many American documents are clearly related to biblical precepts. The following is a listing of some of the more famous ones, along with their biblical counterparts.

1. "We hold these truths to be self-evident, that all men are created equal, that they are endowed by their Creator with certain inalienable rights, that among these are life, liberty and the pursuit of happiness" (Declaration of Independence).
"Have we not all one Father? Has not one God created us? Why should we be faithless to each other, profaning the covenant of our ancestors" (Malachi 2:10).
2. "We, the people of the United States, in order to form a more perfect union, establish justice, insure domestic tranquility, provide for the common defense, promote the general welfare, and secure the blessings of liberty to ourselves and our posterity, do ordain and establish a Constitution for the United States of America" (United States Constitution).

"Justice, justice, shall you pursue, that you may thrive in the land which the Lord your God gives you" (Deuteronomy 16:20).

3. "Congress shall make no law respecting an establishment of religion, or prohibiting the free exercise thereof; or abridging the freedom of speech, or of the press; or the right of the people to assemble, and to petition the government for a redress of grievances" (The Bill of Rights).

"Proclaim liberty throughout the land, for all of its inhabitants" (Leviticus 25:10).

4. "Of all the dispositions and habits which lead to political prosperity, religion and morality are indispensable supports. . . . Where is the security for property, for reputation, for life, if the sense of religious obligation desert the oaths which are the instruments of investigation in courts of justice? And let us with caution indulge the supposition that morality can be maintained without religion" (George Washington, Farewell Address).

"It has been told to you, O man, what is good, and what God requires of you: to act justly, to love mercy and to walk humbly with your God" (Micah 6:8).

5. "For happily the government of the United States which gives to bigotry no sanction, to persecution no assistance, requires only that they who live under its protection should demean themselves as good citizens in giving it on all occasions their effectual support" (George Washington, Letter to Newport Synagogue).

"Righteousness raises a nation to honor, but sin is disgraceful for any people" (Proverbs 14:34).

6. "We here highly resolve that these dead shall not have died in vain, that this nation, under God, shall have a new birth of freedom, and that government of the

people, by the people, and for the people, shall not perish from the earth" (Abraham Lincoln, Gettysburg Address). "How good and how pleasant it is when brothers live together in unity" (Psalm 133:1).

7. "With malice toward none, with charity for all, with firmness in the right as God gives us to see the right, let us strive to finish the work we are in . . . to do all which may achieve and cherish a just and lasting peace among ourselves, and with all nations" (Abraham Lincoln, Second Inaugural Address).

"Let justice roll on like a mighty river, righteousness like a never-ending stream" (Amos 5:26).

Angels

There are a myriad of references to angels in the Bible. They appear in a variety of forms, sometimes as humans and sometimes in other shapes. They can often speak, sit, stand, walk, have weapons, ride horses, or descend from heaven on a ladder. Their functions include worshipping God, singing God's praises, acting as go-betweens, announcing forthcoming events, guarding various places, transmitting revelations to prophets, and carrying out a divine message. Here is a cross section of angel appearances in the Bible:

1. **Abraham's Angel**. In an amazing tale of suspense, Abraham is called upon by God to sacrifice his beloved son Isaac. Abraham ascends Mount Moriah, places his son Isaac on the altar, and picks up his knife. It is then that an angel of the Lord calls to him from heaven, exhorting him not to lift his hand against the boy (Genesis 22:11–12). Abraham has passed the ultimate test of faith, and Isaac's life is saved.

2. **The Angel at the Burning Bush**. Early in Moses' career, he experiences the wondrous and commanding

presence of God while tending sheep. An angel of God appears to him in a blazing fire out of a bush that is not consumed. It is only after Moses realizes that this is a special bush that God directly speaks to him. This story (Exodus 3:1–6) provides us with the first theophany (revelation of God) to Moses.

3. **Balaam's Angel**. In this remarkable tale, Balaam, a false prophet sent by the King of Moab to curse the Israelites, is found riding a talking donkey who is able to perceive an angel of God. The angel speaks to Balaam, chastising him for hitting the donkey so many times. The main burden of this miraculous biblical tale is not the speaking of the donkey but the ability of the donkey to see the angel, contrasted to the evil Balaam who looks and yet is blind. Over and against both of them stands God, who is in control of both (Chapter 22).

4. **Cherubim**. These angels appear for the first time as guardians of the garden of Eden after Adam and Eve are expelled: "To the east of the garden of Eden God placed the cherubim" (Genesis 3:24). The purpose of these angelic beings was to guard the way to the Tree of Life.

5. **Daniel's Angel**. In Daniel 6:21–23, God's angel rescues Daniel from the mouth of lions.

6. **Ezekiel's Angels**. Ezekiel was the first prophet to live and prophesy in exile. In one of his most remarkable visions, he sees the Divine Throne-Chariot of God Himself. Out of a whirlwind came four-faced living creatures, the bodies of angelic beings some of whom have faces that resemble those of various animals. The creatures gallop to and fro with the speed of lightning (Ezekiel 1).

7. **Gideon's Angel**. Gideon, an Israelite judge, is known for his decisive victory over the Midianites. Prior

to this battle, he has an encounter with an angel, who assures him that God is with him. The angelic encounter gives Gideon the strength to carry out his mission (Judges 6:11–14).

8. **Hagar's Angels**. Hagar, the Egyptian maidservant of Sarah, appears in several early stories in the Book of Genesis. When she conceives, she becomes contemptuous of Sarah, who in turn abuses her until she flees into the desert. There, by a spring, Hagar encounters an angel who exhorts her to return, giving her a favorable oracle concerning her future son who will become known as Ishmael.

9. **Isaiah's Angels**. Early in his life, Isaiah, the first major prophet, receives a divine calling. While sitting in the Temple, Isaiah hears angels singing the words "holy, holy, holy is *Adonai Tzevao't*, the whole earth is full of God's glory" (Isaiah 6).

10. **Jacob's Ladder**. Ostensibly to find himself a wife from among his own kinsmen, but actually trying to escape the wrath of his brother Esau, Jacob sets out for the land whence his mother had come. He lies down to spend the night under the open sky, and dreams a dream. In it, a ladder is set on the ground, its top reaches to the sky, and angels of God are going up and down on it (Genesis 28:12–17). This is followed by God's revelation that Jacob will be protected wherever he goes, and that he will be brought back to the Promised Land.

11. **Joshua's Angel**. When the children of Israel finally reach the Promised Land after forty years in the desert, Joshua takes over as commander-in-chief. He has a vision of an angel disguised as a man, who tells him to remove his sandals because the land upon which he is standing is holy (Joshua 5:13–15).

12. **Manoah's Angel**. Manoah was the father of Samson, whose birth is foretold by an angel in Chapter 13 of the Book of Judges. Here the angel of God acts as God's messenger, bearing the message that the son to be born shall be raised as a Nazirite, totally consecrated to God.

13. **Wrestling with an Angel**. As Jacob approaches his homeland, the fear of his brother Esau revives in him. As he rises up that night, he is left alone to experience a crisis in his own personal spiritual history. An unknown adversary, generally interpreted to be God's angel, wrestles with him. Jacob is victorious, and is told that his name shall no longer be Jacob, but Israel (Genesis 32:25–31).

14. **Zechariah's Angel of the Lord and the Heavenly Horses**. For the first time in the Bible, angels in the Book of Zechariah appear to take on an independent life all of their own. In Zechariah 1:8–17, an angel of the Lord acts as an interpreter for Zechariah, instructing him to tell the people that God's angel will soon be manifested toward all of the nations that so cruelly oppressed Israel.

Animals

There are some 120 names of animals in the Bible, mammals, fish, birds, and reptiles being well represented. Here is a cross section of the animals of the Bible, with a reference for each.

English Name	Hebrew Name	Reference
Addax	*Yachmoor*	Deuteronomy 14:5
Ass	*Chamor*	Genesis 12:16
Bat	*Atalef*	Leviticus 11:19
Bear	*Dov*	I Samuel 17:34–37
Bee	*Devorah*	Deuteronomy 1:44
Beetle	*Tola'at*	Deuteronomy 28:39
Bison	*Te'o*	Deuteronomy 14:15
Buffalo	*Meri*	II Samuel 6:13
Camel	*Gamal*	Genesis 12:16
Cattle	*Bakar*	Genesis 13:15
Chameleon	*Teenshemet*	Leviticus 11:30
Cobra	*Peten*	Deuteronomy 32:33
Crane	*Agoor*	Isaiah 38:14
Cricket	*Tzelatzal*	Deuteronomy 28:42
Crocodile	*Taneen*	Jeremiah 51:34
Deer	*Yachmoor*	Deuteronomy 14:5

English Name	Hebrew Name	Reference
Dog	*Kelev*	Exodus 22:30
Dove	*Yonah*	Genesis 8:8
Eagle	*Ayeet*	Genesis 15:11
Earthworm	*Tola'at*	Isaiah 14:11
Fish	*Dag*	Jonah 2:1
Flea	*Parosh*	I Samuel 24:14
Fly	*Zevuv*	Isaiah 7:18
Fox	*Shual*	Lamentations 5:18
Frog	*Tzefardaya*	Exodus 7:27
Gazelle	*Tzvee*	Deuteronomy 12:15
Goat	*Ayz*	Leviticus 7:23
Goose	*Barboor*	I Kings 5:3
Grasshopper	*Chargol*	Leviticus 11:22
Gull	*Shachaf*	Leviticus 11:16
Hare	*Arnevet*	Leviticus 11:6
Hawk	*Naytz*	Leviticus 11:16
Hippopotamus	*Behaymot*	Job 40:15
Horse	*Soos*	Exodus 9:3
Ibex	*Ya'el*	Psalm 104:18
Leopard	*Namer*	Isaiah 11:6
Lion	*Aryeh*	Genesis 49:9
Lizard	*Lita'ah*	Leviticus 11:30
Locust	*Arbeh*	Exodus 10:11
Maggot	*Reema*	Exodus 16:24
Monkey	*Kof*	I Kings 10:22
Mouse	*Achbar*	Leviticus 11:29
Nightingale	*Zamir*	Song of Songs 2:12
Ostrich	*Ya'ayn*	Lamentations 4:3
Owl	*Teenshemet*	Leviticus 11:18
Ox	*Re'aym*	Numbers 23:22
Partridge	*Chaglah*	Numbers 26:33
Peacock	*Tookee*	I Kings 10:22
Quail	*Selav*	Exodus 16:13
Rat	*Choled*	Leviticus 11:29
Scorpion	*Akrav*	Deuteronomy 8:15
Sheep	*Tzone*	Genesis 4:2

English Name	Hebrew Name	Reference
Snake	*Nachash*	Genesis 3:1
Spider	*Akaveesh*	Isaiah 59:5
Stork	*Chasidah*	Leviticus 11:19
Swine	*Chazeer*	Leviticus 11:7
Viper	*Tzefah*	Isaiah 14:29
Vulture	*Peres*	Leviticus 11:13
Wasp	*Tzeera*	Exodus 23:28
Whale	*Leevyatan*	Psalm 104:26
Wolf	*Ze'ev*	Isaiah 11:6

Best Dressed

Although it is not common to think of biblical characters as being clothes conscious, there are numerous examples of the importance of clothing to a variety of biblical personalities. Here is a cross section of some of the Bible's best-dressed people:

1. **Adam and Eve** were clothed by God, who provided both of them with garments of skin, better suited for the rough life in front of them than the apron of leaves they were wearing (Genesis 3:21).
2. **Ezekiel the Prophet** was described as wearing an outfit that included shoes of badger's skins, bracelets, a necklace, earrings, a jewel on the forehead, and a beautiful crown (Ezekiel 16:10–13).
3. The **High Priest** may have been the best-dressed person in the Bible. His main garment, called the *ephod*, was made of a fine linen of gold, blue, and purple. Golden bells decorated the hem of the *ephod*. Over this garment the High Priest wore a breastplate that held twelve gems, each with the name of one of the twelve tribes. Around

17

his head he wore a miter with a gold plate bearing the words "Holiness to the Lord" (Exodus 28:36).

4. The **Israelites** had such fine accoutrements that their garments never got old and their shoes never wore out, although they wandered in the wilderness for forty years (Deuteronomy 29:5).

5. The **Israelites** wore garments adorned with fringes with threads of blue, in keeping with the biblical command to put fringes on the corners of their garments, the sight of which was to remind them to observe all of the religious commandments (Numbers 15:38–39).

6. **Jeremiah** was often dressed in crimson clothing with golden ornaments (Jeremiah 4:30).

7. **Job** wore an earring of gold (Job 42:11).

8. **Joseph** wore a coat of many colors, which was given to him by his father Jacob. This coat made him the envy of his brothers, who ultimately stripped Joseph of the coat and sold him into slavery (Genesis 37:3–28).

9. In the Book of Judges the **Midianite camels** wore necklaces (Judges 8:24–26).

10. The **Phoenicians** wore fine Egyptian linen garments and purple or blue robes (Ezekiel 12:16).

Bible Commentators

Over the centuries numerous people have added their personal commentary to the Bible. The following is a summary of these commentators:

ANCIENT

Mechilta. Oldest rabbinic commentary on Exodus

Midrash. Ancient homiletical expositions of the Torah and the Five Scrolls

Philo Judaeus. Renowned Jewish philosopher in Alexandria, author of allegorical commentaries on The Five Books of Moses

Septuagint. The Greek translation of the Bible made by the Jews in Egypt

Sifra. Oldest rabbinic commentary on Leviticus

Sifri. Oldest rabbinic commentary on Numbers and Deuteronomy

MEDIEVAL

Abraham Ibn Ezra. Spanish biblical commentator
Chizkuni. Thirteenth-century French commentator
David Kimchi. French-Spanish exegete
Don Isaac Abarbanel. Spanish biblical commentator
Joseph Bechor Shor. Twelfth-century French commentator
Obadiah Sforno. Italian commentator
Rashi. Greatest of all the biblical commentators, known for his literal interpretation of the Bible

MODERN

Israel Abrahams. Anglo-Jewish commentator
David Altshul. Wrote popular commentaries on prophetic books
Umberto Cassuto. Italian-Jewish commentator
Samson Raphael Hirsch. German commentator
Marcus Jastrow. American Bible scholar
Isaac Leeser. American Bible translator
S. D. Luzzatto. Italian Hebraist and commentator
M. L. Malbim. Russian commentator
Leopold Zunz. Edited and translated the Bible that is most used among German-speaking Jews

Bible Portion Summaries

The first of the Five Books of Moses begins with the creation of the world out of the void. It ends with the last days of Moses. Each week a different *sidrah* (Torah portion) is read on Saturday morning in traditional synagogues. Here is a list of the Torah portions for the entire year and a brief summary of each of their contents.

GENESIS

Contents

The creation of the world. The patriarchs—Abraham, Isaac, and Jacob. Jacob and his sons go down to Egypt. Jacob blesses his sons before his death.

> *Bereishit* (1:1–6:8) The world is created in six days.
> *Noah* (6:9–11:32) A flood destroys the world. God's rainbow promises that the world will never again be destroyed in its entirety.

Lekh Lekha (12:1–17:27) Abraham leaves Mesopotamia for the Promised Land.

Vayera (18:1–22:24) Abraham welcomes three angels into his tent and learns that his wife Sarah will give birth to a son.

Chayyei Sarah (23:1–25:18) Eliezer finds a suitable wife, Rebekah, for Abraham's son Isaac.

Toledot (25:19–28:9) The birth of Esau and Jacob. Isaac blesses Jacob.

Vayetze (28:10–32:3) God appears to Jacob in a dream. Jacob works fourteen years and marries Leah and Rachel.

Vayishlach (32:4–36:43) Jacob and Esau reunite after twenty years. Rachel dies and is buried in Bethlehem.

Vayeshev (37:1–40:23) Joseph's brothers strip him of his coat of many colors and throw him into a pit.

Mikketz (41:1–44:17) Joseph successfully interprets Pharaoh's dreams. Joseph is appointed viceroy.

Vayigash (44:18–47:27) Joseph reveals himself to his brothers, who are dumbfounded.

Vayechi (47:28–50:26) Jacob blesses his sons. Joseph dies at end of book at age 110.

EXODUS

Contents

The Israelites are enslaved in Egypt. Moses receives the Ten Commandments. The Israelites build a tabernacle.

Weekly Portions

Shemot (1:1–6:1) Moses is saved by Pharaoh's daughter. God appears to Moses at the burning bush.

Vayera (6:2–9:35) God brings plagues upon the Egyptians. Pharaoh's heart hardens and he refuses to let the Israelites go.

Bo (10:1–13:16) Egyptian firstborn children are slain by God. The Israelites hastily leave Egypt and bake *matzah* from unleavened dough.

Beshallach (13:17–17:16) The waters of the Red Sea divide to make a path for the Israelites.

Yitro (18:1–20:23) Jethro, Moses' father-in-law, advises him to appoint judges so as to ease his burden. Moses receives the Ten Commandments on Mount Sinai.

Mishpatim (21:1–24:18) Moses instructs the Israelites in the Law.

Terumah (25:1–27:19) The tabernacle is constructed.

Tetzaveh (27:20–30:10) Aaron and his sons are put in charge of the *menorah*. The priestly garments are described in great detail.

Ki Tissa (30:11–34:35) The Israelites build a golden calf; when Moses sees it he shatters the tablets containing the Ten Commandments.

Vayakhel (35:1–38:20) The people bring an array of gifts for the tabernacle until they are told to stop.

Pekudei (38:21–40:38) The cloud of glory covers the completed tabernacle as the Israelites stand in the distance.

LEVITICUS

Contents

The priestly code; the rules pertaining to sacrifices, diet, and morality; and the Land of Israel and festivals are discussed.

Weekly Portions

Vayikra (1:1–5:26) God reveals the sacrificial laws.

Tzav (6:1–8:36) Moses anoints Aaron and his sons as priests.

Shemini (9:1–11:47) Laws describing kosher and non-kosher animals are enumerated.

Tazria (12:1–13:59) Cleanliness and uncleanliness are defined in relation to childbirth and leprosy.

Metzora (14:1–15:33) The laws for the purification of the leper after he has healed are discussed.

Acharei Mot (16:1–18:30) Aaron's sons die. Aaron chooses by lot a goat and a scapegoat.

Kedoshim (19:1–20:27) More laws are set forth, including "Love your neighbor as yourself."

Emor (21:1–24:23) Festival seasons are described in detail.

Behar (25:1–26:2) The sabbatical and jubilee years are discussed.

Bechukkotai (26:3–27:34) The punishment for rejecting God's covenant is discussed.

NUMBERS

Contents

The census. More statutes and laws. Adventures of the Hebrews en route to Canaan through the desert.

Weekly Portions

Bamidbar (1:1–4:20) Description of the Israelites' encampments during their journeys through the desert.

Naso (4:21–7:89) Regulations concerning Nazirites and the threefold priestly benediction.

Behaalotekha (8:1–12:16) Kindling of the *menorah*. Seventy elders are delegated to serve under Moses.

Shelach Lekha (13:1–15:41) Twelve spies are dispatched to survey the land of Canaan. Two of the spies return with a positive report.

Korach (16:1–18:32) Korach refuses to accept the leadership of Moses and Aaron. He and his assembly are killed by an earthquake.

Chukkat (19:1–22:1) The laws regarding the red heifer are enumerated. Moses strikes the rock and water gushes forth.

Balak (22:2–25:9) Balak, king of Moab, sends Bilaam to curse the Israelites. Instead, Bilaam gives his blessing to them.

Pinchas (25:10–30:1) The daughters of Zelophechad are given their father's inheritance. Moses chooses Joshua as his successor.

Mattot (30:2–32:42) Moses informs the tribal heads regarding the laws of vowing.

Masei (33:1–36:13) The detailed account of the various way stations on the Israelites' route to the Promised Land. Reference is made to the cities of refuge.

DEUTERONOMY

Contents

A recapitulation of the laws with some additions. Moses addresses the children of Israel and presents them with some warnings.

Weekly Portions

Devarim (1:1–3:22) Moses explains and interprets the law to the people.

Va'et'chanan (3:23–7:11) The Ten Commandments are repeated, with slight variations. The cities of refuge are mentioned. The first section of the *Shema* is begun with "You shall love the Lord your God."

Ekev (7:12–11:25) The *Shema* continues with the second paragraph, which deals with the theme of reward and punishment.

Re'eh (11:26–16:17) Moses continues his address, telling the people that obedience will bring them blessings, whereas disobedience will bring them curses.

Shoftim (16:18–21:9) Moses warns the people against idolatry. He also reminds the people of the importance of pursuing justice.

Ki Tetze (21:10–25:19) Moses reviews a variety of laws intended to strengthen family life and human decency in Israel. These laws refer to lost property, the educational responsibility of parents to their children, and kindness to animals, among other things.

Ki Tavo (26:1–29:8) The laws of tithing and first fruits are discussed.

Nitzavim (29:9–30:20) Moses continues his farewell speech and God tells the people to choose life.

Vayelekh (31:1–30) Joshua is appointed successor to Moses. Moses completes the writing of the Torah.

Haazinu (32:1–52) Moses' farewell song, a beautiful poem in which he calls upon heaven and earth to witness God's dependability.

Vezot HaBerakhah (33:1–34:12) Moses' final blessing poem and the report of Moses' death on Mount Nebo. Israel now turns to Joshua for leadership.

Biblical Firsts

As the first book of recorded history in the west, the Bible contains numerous examples of first occurrences. Here is a summary of Bible firsts:

First case of disrespectful behavior to parents	Ham (Genesis 9:22)
First Commandment	"Be fruitful and multiply" (Genesis 1:28)
First farmer	Cain (Genesis 4:3)
First firemaker	Adam (Genesis Rabbah 9:2)
First to have parents	Cain (Genesis 4:1)
First Jew	Abraham
First King of Israel	Saul (I Samuel 10:1)
First King of Judah	David (II Samuel 2:4)
First man to be sick	Jacob (Genesis 32:32)
First man to wear a mask	Moses (Exodus 34:35)
First matchmaker	Eliezer (Genesis 24:12)
First *matzah* baker	Lot (Genesis 19:3)
First messenger	Raven (Genesis 8:7)
First person to hold a beauty contest	King Ahasuerus (Esther 2:1)
First pseudonym	Esther, name used by Hadassah (Esther 2:7)

27

First real-estate transaction	Abraham and Efron (Genesis 23:16)
First to receive eviction notice	Adam and Eve
First recorded dream	Abimelech (Genesis 20:3)
First recorded stutterer	Moses (Exodus 4:10)
First shipbuilder	Noah (Genesis 6:14)
First skyscraper	Tower of Babel (Genesis 11:1–8)
First vintager	Noah (Genesis 9:20)
First war	War of the Kings of the North (Genesis 14:1–10)
First woman whose consent for marriage was asked	Rebekah (Genesis 24:58)
First women to demand property rights	Daughters of Zelophechad (Numbers 36:2)
First world traveler	Cain (Genesis 4:16)
First wrestler	Jacob (Genesis 33:25)

Bible Statistics and Miscellany

The Bible has more than 773,000 words and 3.5 million letters. There are thirty-nine books in the Jewish Bible, 929 chapters, and 23,214 verses.

MASORETIC STATISTICS

The Masoretes were a group of scribes who catalogued and numbered the total number of verses, *sedrot* (weekly Bible portions), and chapters of each of the Five Books of Moses. Here is a summary of the findings:

Book of Genesis:

> Total number of verses is 1,534.
> Total number of *sedrot* is 12.
> Total number of smaller divisions according to the triennial cycle is 43.
> Total number of chapters is 50.

Book of Exodus

Total number of verses is 1,209.
Total number of *sedrot* is 11.
Total number of smaller divisions is 29.
Total number of chapters is 40.

Book of Leviticus

Total number of verses is 859.
Total number of *sedrot* is 10.
Total number of smaller divisions is 23.
Total number of chapters is 27.

Book of Numbers

Total number of verses is 1,288.
Total number of *sedrot* is 10.
Total number of smaller divisions is 32.
Total number of chapters is 36.

Book of Deuteronomy

Total number of verses is 955.
Total number of sedrot is 11.
Total number of smaller divisions is 27.
Total number of chapters is 34.

Total number of verses in the Five Books of Moses is 5,845.

STATISTICS OF BIBLICAL NAMES

The following is a summary of the number of times certain names are mentioned in the Five Books of Moses:

Aaron: 301
Asher: 20
Balak: 40
Benjamin: 31
Bilaam: 55
Children of Israel: 364
Dan: 26
Ephraim: 26
Esau: 80
Gad: 33
Gershon: 19
Isaac: 98
Ishmael: 17
Issachar: 19
Jacob: 202
Joseph: 173
Joshua: 28
Judah: 48
Leah: 33
Levi: 41
Lot: 32
Moses: 662
Naftali: 19
Noah: 40
Pharaoh: 210
Rachel: 44
Rebekah: 30

Reuben: 45
Sarah: 38
Simeon: 25
Zebulun: 19

STATISTICS OF HEBREW LETTERS

Aleph: 42,377
Beit: 38,218
Gimel: 29,537
Dalet: 32,530
Hey: 47,754
Vov: 76,922
Zayin: 22,867
Chet: 23,447
Tet: 11,052
Yud: 66,420
Chaf: 37,272
    Final chaf: 10,981
Lamed: 41,517
Mem: 52,805
    Final Mem: 24,973
Nun: 32,977
    Final Nun: 8,719
Samach: 13,580
Ayin: 20,175
Pey: 20,750
    Final Pey: 1,975
Tzaddi: 16,950
    Final Tzaddi: 4,872
Kuf: 22,972

Reish: 22,147
Shin: Sin: 32,148
Tav: 36,140

TEN TORAH PORTIONS
WITH THE MOST VERSES

Naso: 176
Pinchas: 164
Bamidbar: 159
Vayishlach: 154
Noah: 153
Vayetze: 148
Vayera: 147
Bereishit: 146
Mikketz: 146
Ki Tissa: 139

LONGEST VERSE IN THE BIBLE

The longest verse in the Bible appears in the Book of Esther
(8:9), which has forty-three words in Hebrew.

BIBLE MISCELLANY

1. The middle verse of the Torah is Leviticus 8:8: "He
put the breastplate on him, and put into the breastplate the
Urim and Thummim."

2. The middle words of the Torah are "*darosh doresh*", found in Leviticus 10:16.

3. All the Hebrew letters of the alphabet are found in Esther 3:13.

4. The shortest verses in the Bible are I Chronicles 1:1 and I Chronicles 1:25, each with only three words and nine letters.

5. The Bible's shortest prayer, consisting of five words, is found in Numbers 12:3, recited by Moses for his sister Miriam, whom God had afflicted with leprosy: *el na refah na lah* ("Please God, heal her").

6. The shortest chapter in the Bible is Psalm 117.

7. The longest chapter in the Bible is Psalm 119, which has 176 verses.

8. The only two books in the Bible that do not mention God's name are the Song of Songs and the Book of Esther.

9. The only two biblical men that never died in the Bible were Enoch, who the Bible said "walked with God" (Genesis 5:24) and Elijah, who was carried by a whirlwind into heaven (II Kings 2:11).

10. Seven people in the Bible lived more than 900 years: Adam lived 930 years (Genesis 5:5), Seth lived 912 years (Genesis 5:8), Enoch lived 905 years (Genesis 5:11), Cain lived 910 years (Genesis 5:14), Jared lived 962 years (Genesis 5:20), Methuselah lived 969 years (Genesis 5:27), and Noah lived 950 years (Genesis 9:29).

11. The largest general number in the Bible is "thousands of millions." Rebekah's family blessed her by saying "be thou the mother of thousands of millions" (Genesis 24:60).

12. The longest book in the Bible is Psalms, with 150 chapters and a total of 2,461 verses.

13. The shortest book in the Bible is Obadiah, which is comprised of twenty-one verses and only one chapter.

14. The Bible's longest word is *mahershalalchashbaz* (Isaiah 8:3), which is actually a coined term consisting of four Hebrew words meaning "speedy booty, sudden spoils."

15. The commandment to observe the Sabbath in Exodus 20:11 refers to the seventh day of the week. It begins in Hebrew with the letter *zayin*, the seventh letter of the alphabet. It appears in the seventh verse of the Ten Commandments and it proclaims rest for seven classes of creatures.

16. There are certain words or word forms occurring only once in the Bible, called *hapax legomena*. There are 414 absolute ones in the Bible, plus an additional 887 other unique forms that, however, are traceable to familiar roots or stems. The Books of Joshua, Obadiah, and Haggai are the only ones not having any, whereas the most occur in the Books of Isaiah and Job, having sixty in each.

17. The Bible is a collection of thirty-nine books. In the Bible itself, several other books are mentioned. They include the following: the Book of Wars (Numbers 21:14), the Book of Jashar (Joshua 3:10), the Chronicles of David (I Chronicles 27:24), the Book of Gad (I Chronicles 29:29), the Book of the Prophet Iddo (II Chronicles 13:22), the Book of Natan (I Chronicles 29:29), the Book of Remembrance (Malachi 3:16), and the Book of Life (Daniel 12:1).

Biblical Names

Today biblical names are used with great frequency in the naming of children. Here is a list of some biblical names that are commonly used in English nowadays:

1. **Aaron**, meaning "messenger" or "mountain." He was the brother of Moses and Miriam, and the founder of the Israelite priestly dynasty (Exodus Chapter 4).
2. **Abigail**, with variants including Abby and Gail. The name means "my father's joy." Abigail was an early follower of David before he became king (I Samuel 25:14–42).
3. **Abraham**, meaning "father of a mighty nation." Abraham was Israel's first patriarch (Genesis 11:26–25:10).
4. **Adam**, meaning "man" or "red earth." He was the first human being created by God, on the sixth day of creation (Genesis 1–3).
5. **Amos**, meaning "burdened" or "troubled." Originally a shepherd, Amos was a minor prophet who lived in the time of the Judean King Uzziah (Book of Amos).

6. **Benjamin**, meaning "son of my right hand." He was the youngest of Jacob's twelve sons by Rachel (Genesis 35:16–50:16).

7. **Dan**, meaning "he judged." He was the fifth son of Jacob by Bilhah, Rachel's handmaiden (Genesis 30:6–50:16).

8. **Daniel**, meaning "God is my judge." He was an Israelite prophet who as a youngster was taken to the court of the Babylonian King Nebuchadnezzar in order to be taught Chaldean culture (Book of Daniel).

9. **David**, meaning "beloved." He was the second King of Israel (I Samuel 16–II Samuel).

10. **Deborah**, meaning "swarm of bees." She was both a judge and a prophet of Israel (Judges 4, 5).

11. **Dinah**, meaning "judgement." The only recorded daughter of Jacob, by his wife Leah, she was raped by Shechem (Genesis 30:21, 34).

12. **Elijah**, meaning "the Lord is my God." He was a prophet, who, according to tradition, did not die and under various disguises continues to accompany Israel in her exile (I Kings 17:1–2, II Kings 2:11).

13. **Elisheva**, with Elizabeth as a variant, meaning "the oath of God." She was the wife of Aaron (Exodus 6:23).

14. **Emanuel**, meaning "God is with us." He was the child prophesied by Isaiah to be born to Ahaz (Isaiah 7:14–17).

15. **Esther**, meaning "a star." She was a Persian Jewish woman who saved the Jews from the evil decree of Haman (Book of Esther).

16. **Ezra**, meaning "God helps." He was a scribe who chronicled and supervised the return of the Babylonian exiled Jews (Book of Ezra).

17. **Hanna,** meaning "grace," with variants Ann, Anita and Nancy. She was the mother of the prophet Samuel (I Samuel 1–2).

18. **Isaac,** meaning "laughter." He was the son of Abraham and the Israelites' second patriarch (Genesis 21–35:28).

19. **Jacob,** meaning "held by the heel" or "supplanter." He was the son of Isaac and Rebekah, twin brother of Esau, and the third of the Jewish patriarchs (Genesis 25:23–49:33).

20. **Joel,** meaning "God is willing." He was a minor prophet who preached in Judea (Book of Joel).

21. **Jonathan,** meaning "God has given." He was the first son of King Saul and loyal friend to David (I Samuel 14–15).

22. **Joseph,** meaning "he will increase." He was the favored son of Jacob, known for his coat of many colors (Genesis 37:1–50:26).

23. **Michael,** meaning "who is like God?" He was one of the four archangels of God (Daniel 10:13–21).

24. **Miriam,** meaning "bitter sea." She was a prophet and sister of Moses and Aaron (Numbers 12:10–15, 20:1).

25. **Rachel,** meaning "ewe." She was the daughter of Rebekah's brother Laban and the younger sister of Leah (Genesis 29–35).

26. **Rebekah,** meaning "to tie" or "to bind." She was the wife of Isaac and mother of Jacob and Esau (Genesis 24–28).

27. **Ruth,** meaning "friendship." She was the daughter-in-law of Naomi and a Moabite woman (Book of Ruth).

28. **Samuel**, meaning "God has heard." He was a prophet and last of the Israelite judges (I and II Samuel).

29. **Sarah**, meaning "princess." She was the wife of Abraham and the Israelites' first matriarch (Genesis 11:29–23:1).

Biblical Phrases in Everyday Speech

A goodly number of biblical phrases continue to be used today in everyday speech. Here is a cross section of some of the more notable ones:

1. "I am escaped with **the skin of my teeth**" (Job 19:20).

2. **"Am I my brother's keeper?"** (Genesis 4:9).

3. "And you shall eat **the fat of the land**" (Genesis 45:18).

4. "He that **spareth the rod hateth his son**" (Proverbs 13:24).

5. **"Pride goes before destruction"** (Proverbs 16:18).

6. "A man has no better thing under the sun, than to **eat, drink, and be merry**" (Ecclesiastes 8:15).

7. "The nations are as **a drop in a bucket**" (Isaiah 40:15).

8. "I am **holier than thou**" (Isaiah 65:5).

9. "Can the Ethiopian change his skin or **the leopard change his spots?**" (Jeremiah 13:23).

Books of the Bible and their Meanings

There are thirty-nine books of the Jewish Bible. Here are their names, their Hebrew names, and their meanings:

Book	Hebrew Name	Meaning
Amos	Amos	Burden
Chronicles	Divrei HaYamim	Words of the days
Daniel	Daniel	God is judge
Deuteronomy	Devarim	Words
Ecclesiastes	Kohelet	Provider
Esther	Esther	Star
Exodus	Shemot	Names
Ezekiel	Yechezkel	God makes strong
Ezra	Ezra	Help
Genesis	Bereishit	In the beginning
Habakkuk	Chabbakuk	Beloved one
Haggai	Chaggai	Festive one
Hosea	Hoshea	Salvation
Isaiah	Yeshayahu	God saves
Jeremiah	Yirmiyahu	God lifts us
Job	Eeyov	Hated

Book	Hebrew Name	Meaning
Joel	Yoel	God is willing
Jonah	Yonah	Dove
Joshua	Yehoshua	God saves
Judges	Shoftim	Judges
Kings	Malachim	Kings
Lamentations	Eicha	How
Leviticus	Vayikra	And He called
Malachi	Malachi	My messenger
Micah	Micha	Who is like God
Nahum	Nachum	Comforter
Nehemiah	Nechemiah	God is consolation
Numbers	Bamidbar	In the desert
Obadiah	Ovadiah	Worshiper of God
Psalms	Tehillim	Praise
Proverbs	Mishle	Proverbs
Ruth	Rute	Female friend
Samuel	Shmuel	Heard by God
Song of Songs	Shir HaShirim	Song of Songs
Zachariah	Zechariah	God is remembered
Zephaniah	Tzephania	God hides

Books of the Apocrypha

The Apocrypha is a series of books, written during the last centuries B.C.E., that were excluded from the Bible. Some of the books were written in Greek and modeled after the books of the Bible. Here is a summary of the Apocryphal books:

1. **Book of Baruch**. A book of wisdom written by Baruch, a scribe and the secretary of the Prophet Jeremiah.

2. **Book of Tobit**. The miraculous story of a man named Tobit and his son Tobias.

3. **Bel and the Dragon**. The story of Daniel, who fought the idol Bel and the mythical god Dragon. The story also tells of Daniel's taming of the lions.

4. **Epistle of Jeremiah**. The story of Jeremiah, who warns the exiles against worshipping idols.

5. **I Maccabees**. The story of the Jews from the time of King Antiochus until the death of Simon Maccabee.

6. **II Maccabees**. The history of the Jews from Seleucus IV until the death of Nicanor.

7. **III Maccabees**. The story of God's punishment of Ptolemy IV for polluting the Temple sanctuary.

8. **IV Maccabees**. A book of stoicism.

9. **Prayer of Manasseh**. The story of Manasseh, king of Judea and the son of Hezekiah.

10. **Song of the Three Children**. The story of Azarias, Chanamia, and Mishoel, who were saved from death in a furnace.

11. **Susanna**. The story of Susanna, who was falsely accused of adultery by the elders but was eventually vindicated.

12. **Third Book of Ezra**. The story of Zerubabel, who received permission from King Darius to visit Judea as the victor's reward in a debate over what was the strongest thing on earth. (He had said that women were the strongest things on earth.)

13. **Wisdom of Ben Sira**. This book, written by Ben Sira, contains many words of wisdom about religion.

14. **Wisdom of Solomon**. A book of philosophy about God, author unknown.

Capital Punishment

There is little evidence to show that capital punishment was carried on to any great extent in biblical times. The following specific transgressions, however, are mentioned in the Bible as punishable by death and as offenses against God, humans, and morality.

1. Adultery (Leviticus 20:10)

2. Apostasy (Deuteronomy 13:2)

3. Bestiality (Exodus 22:18)

4. Blasphemy (Leviticus 24:16)

5. Idolatry (Deuteronomy 17:2)

6. Incest (Leviticus 20:11)

7. Licentiousness (Leviticus 21:9)

8. Manstealing (Exodus 21:16)

9. Murder (Exodus 21:12)

10. Rape of a betrothed woman (Deuteronomy 22:25)

11. Sacrifice of children (Leviticus 20:2)

12. Sodomy (Leviticus 20:13)

13. Striking or cursing a parent (Exodus 21:15)

14. Witchcraft and sorcery (Exodus 22:17)

15. Working on the Sabbath (Numbers 15:35)

Census

The term *census* derives from the ancient Roman institution of registering adult males and their property for purposes of taxation, military levy, and the determination of political status. The Bible reports that the first census took place at Mount Sinai prior to the end of the first year following the exodus from Egypt (Exodus 40:17). The count was made in connection with the remittance of a half shekel by each male Israelite 20 years of age and older (Exodus 30:12). What follows are some census statistics that occur throughout the Bible.

1. Six hundred thousand people left Egypt on foot in the Exodus (Exodus 12:37).

2. God commanded Moses to number his army by recording every male 20 years of age and older (Numbers 1:1–46). The results were:

Tribe of Reuben—46,500
Tribe of Simeon—59,300
Tribe of Gad—45,650
Tribe of Judah—74,600

Tribe of Issachar—54,400
Tribe of Zebulun—57,400
Half tribe of Ephraim—40,500
Half tribe of Manasseh—32,200
Tribe of Benjamin—35,400
Tribe of Dan—62,700
Tribe of Asher—41,500
Tribe of Naphtali—53,400
Total number of Israelite fighting men—603,550

3. God commanded that a census be taken of the Levites. Moses found 22,000 Levites more than 1 month old (Numbers 3:39).

4. After 24,000 people had died in a plague of judgment, God commanded Moses to take a census of the army. Moses found 601,730 men over 20 years of age (Numbers 26:1–51).

5. The armies of Israel came against the tribe of Benjamin in judgment. A census showed 26,000 Benjamite soldiers and 400,000 from Israel. After the battle, only 600 Benjamite men remained (Judges 20:14–48).

6. Saul numbered the army that had prepared to fight the Ammonites and counted 330,000 men (I Samuel 11:8).

7. David brought God's anger upon Israel by numbering the kingdom. He counted 1,300,000 valiant men who drew the sword (II Samuel 24:1–15).

8. Under King David, the Levites were numbered from the age of 30 years and upward. Their number was 38,000 (I Chronicles 23:3).

9. Solomon numbered all of the aliens in Israel and found 153,600 (II Chronicles 2:17).

10. Ezra brought 42,360 people and 7,337 of their servants back to Jerusalem from Babylon (Ezra 2:64, 65).

Chronology of the Bible

The stories of the Bible start with the creation of the world and end with the return from the Babylonian captivity. According to traditional Jewish calculation, creation took place 3,761 years before the Common Era. One needs only to add to this figure the present calendar year in order to arrive at the age of the world according to the Bible.

The period of time covered in the Bible was computed from genealogies—records of birth and deaths—as mentioned in the early chapters of Genesis and in the Books of Chronicles. There are several differing chronologies for the dates before 700 C.E., as they are uncertain.

Here is the chronology in brief:

From Creation	Event	Before Common Era
1	Creation of world	3761
1–930	Adam	3761–2830
1056–2006	Noah	2704–1754
1656	The flood	2104
1948–2123	Abraham	1812–1637
2023	Leaving of Ur	1737

From Creation	Event	Before Common Era
1958–2085	Sarah	1802–1675
2048–2228	Isaac	1712–1532
2108–2255	Jacob	1652–1505
2199–2309	Joseph	1561–1451
2229	Viceroy in Egypt	1531
2182–2304	Aaron	1578–1456
2188–2308	Moses	1572–1452
2268	The Exodus	1492
2268–2308	In the wilderness	1492–1452
2238–2348	Joshua	1522–1412
2308	Successor to Moses	1452
2390–2470	Period of Judges	1370–1020
2732–2827	The Monarchy	1028–933
3038	Fall of Israel	722
3174	Fall of Jerusalem	586
3316	Return from exile	444

Cities

The following is a listing of some of the cities and towns mentioned in the Bible:

1. **Anatote**: Home of Jeremiah (Jeremiah 1:1).

2. **Arad**: Where men took some of the children of Israel prisoners (Numbers 21:1–2).

3. **Ashdod**: One of the five main Philistine cities, where the ark of the covenant caused the destruction of Dagon the pagan god (I Samuel 5:1–8).

4. **Ashkelon**: An important Philistine city on the coast of the Mediterranean (I Samuel 6:16). Samson slew thirty men in Ashkelon (Judges 14:19).

5. **Ashtarot**: Home of a number of giants (Deuteronomy 1:4).

6. **Beersheba**: The place in southern Israel where Abraham made a covenant with Avimelech and to which Hagar fled (Genesis 21:14, 31).

7. **Bethel**: Abraham worshiped God here (Genesis 12:8). Jacob dreamed his dream of the heavenly ladder at Bethel (Genesis 28:8–19).

8. **Bethlehem**: Rachel's burial place (Genesis 35:15–18) and home of Boaz and Ruth (Book of Ruth).

9. **Bet Peor**: Burial place of Moses (Deuteronomy 4:44–46).

10. **Bet She'an**: Place where the bodies of Saul and Jonathan were nailed to the wall (I Samuel 31:8–13).

11. **Bet Shemesh**: Birthplace of Samson (Judges 13:2–25).

12. **Damascus**: Home of Abraham's faithful servant Eliezer (Genesis 15:2).

13. **Dan**: City in northern Israel marking the northern limit of Israel in the time of the Bible (I Samuel 3:20).

14. **Dotan**: Place where Jacob was sold into slavery (Genesis 37:17).

15. **Ekron**: One of the five main Philistine cities whose leaders rid themselves of the Ark of God (I Samuel 10–12).

16. **Endor**: Place where Saul visited the witch (I Samuel 28:7–14).

17. **Etzion-Gever**: Home of King Solomon's navy (I Kings 9:26).

18. **Gat**: Philistine city, home of Goliath (I Samuel 17:4).

19. **Gaza**: Philistine city that had its main gates along with the gateposts pulled up and carried away by Samson (Judges 16:1–3).

20. **Gerar**: Place where Abraham lied the second time about Sarah (Genesis 20).

21. **Gibeah**: Home of King Saul (I Samuel 10:26).

22. **Gibeon**: Place where the sun stood still (Joshua 10:12–13).

23. **Gilgal**: First stop of the Israelites after they crossed the Jordan River (Joshua 4:19).

24. **Gomorrah**: Wicked city near Sodom that was destroyed by God (Genesis 19:24–25).

25. **Haran**: Home of Rebekah and the home of Jacob for twenty years, where most of his sons were born (Genesis 24:10).

26. **Hazor**: Headquarters of Israel's enemy Sisera (Judges 4:1–2).

27. **Hebron**: Burial place of Sarah, Abraham, Isaac, and Jacob (Genesis 23:2, 25:9, 35:37, 50:13).

28. **Jericho**: Home of Rahab the harlot (Joshua 2). City from which Elijah departed into heaven (II Kings 2:1–5).

29. **Jerusalem**: (see separate entry).

30. **Jezreel**: Place of Jezebel's death (II Kings 9:10).

31. **Joffa**: Place where Jonah attempted to flee from God's command (Jonah 1:3).

32. **Masada**: Place where David hid from Saul (I Samuel 24:22).

33. **Michmash**: Place of Israel's victory over the Philistines (I Samuel 14:1–23).

34. **Mitzpah**: The hometown of Jephthah (Judges 11:34).

35. **Nineveh**: Capital of Assyria where Jonah was sent by God to preach his message of repentance (Jonah 1).

36. **Nob**: Place where David took refuge when he fled from King Saul (I Samuel 21:1).

37. **Ramah**: Home of the parents of Samuel the Prophet (I Samuel 1:19).

38. **Samariah**: Capital city of the Northern Kingdom, built by King Omri (I Kings 16:24).

39. **Shechem**: One of six cities of refuge (Joshua 20:7–8) and place where Joshua gave his farewell address (Joshua 24:1).

40. **Shiloh**: Home of the tabernacle after Israel conquered Palestine (Joshua 18:1).

41. **Sodom**: Place of wickedness that was destroyed in its entirety by God (Genesis 14:21–24).

42. **Tekoah**: Home of a crafty woman who attempted to reconcile David and Absalom (II Samuel 14:2–4).

43. **Tyre**: Home of Hiram, supplier of King Solomon's temple (I Kings 5:1–11).

44. **Ur**: Birthplace of Abraham (Genesis 11:27).

CITIES OF REFUGE

In the Bible one type of crime, an unintentional murder, was punishable by a unique form of imprisonment. The unwitting murderer was permitted to escape the "avenger of blood" (a member of the deceased's family responsible in common law for such revenge) by entering one of the six cities of refuge. These cities were set up not as asylums for people convicted of murder but for the unlucky who murdered by accident. The six cities of refuge, three east and three west of the Jordan River, were:

1. Hebron in southern Judah (Joshua 2:11)

2. Shechem on Mount Ephraim (Joshua 21:21)

3. Kadesh in Galilee (I Chronicles 6:76)

4. Bezer in Moab (Deuteronomy 4:43)

5. Ramot-Gilead (Deuteronomy 4:43)

6. Golan in Bashan (Deuteronomy 4:43)

Clothing

The biblical terms for clothing refer to a variety of items that cover the body for warmth or for reasons of modesty. The terms are also used extensively in figures of speech: "Put on your beautiful garments" (Isaiah 52:1) is a symbol of greatness; "God put on garments of vengeance for clothing" (Isaiah 59:17) is a symbol of revenge.

Here is a cross section of references to clothing in the Bible:

1. Adam and Eve sewed fig leaves together for clothing (Genesis 3:7).

2. God made for Adam and Eve garments of skin and clothed them (Genesis 3:21).

3. During the period of mourning a widow wore a characteristic garment: "She put off from her garments of widowhood" (Genesis 38:14).

4. Prisoners had special clothing: "He changed his prison garments" (II Kings 25:29).

5. Metal or leather helmets and head coverings were used in time of war for protection (I Samuel 17:5).

6. A dress-like garment, apparently with closed seams, was used by both men and women to cover the entire body from the shoulders to the ankles (I Kings 11:30).

7. A tunic, a short, closed garment covering the top part of the body, was worn by both men and women (Genesis 37:3, Leviticus 16:14).

8. A coat, a long outer garment open at the front, was worn in biblical times (I Samuel 15:27).

9. The Israelites were commanded by God to wear clothing with fringes and a thread of blue on the corners of their garments (Numbers 15:37–41). This became the precursor of the modern *tallit* or prayershawl.

10. The King wore special royal apparel to emphasize his special status in the kingdom (Esther 6:8).

11. Wearing a sackcloth was a sign of mourning in biblical times (Jonah 3:5).

12. The Song of Deborah (Judges 5:30) cites dyed garments of embroidery.

13. The chapter describing Samson's wedding feast makes note of thirty linen garments and thirty changes of clothing (Judges 14:12,13).

14. Biblical women often wore veils, a sign of modesty and humility (Genesis 24:65).

15. Isaiah 3:18 contains one of the most extensive lists of clothing and ornaments worn by women in Jerusalem during the middle of the eighth century B.C.E. Unfortunately it is very difficult to identify many of the items in the catalogue of finery.

16. Soldiers wore high boots (Isaiah 9:4).

17. Shoes had symbolic significance in biblical times. The renunciation of levirate marriage obligations involved an elaborate ceremony that included the removal of a shoe (Deuteronomy 25:9). To be "unsandaled" was to

be dispossessed (Deuteronomy 25:10). To cast one's sandals upon property signified possession (Psalm 60:10). Taking off one's shoes at a holy place was a mark of respect (Exodus 3:5). To go without shoes was an outward sign of mourning (II Samuel 15:30).

18. Joseph wore a coat of many colors (Genesis 37:3).

19. High Priests had their own special uniform. The priestly garments as a whole are frequently referred to as holy garments. A total of eight garments is enumerated in the Bible, but only Aaron attired himself in all eight. Of these, the four undergarments are to be worn by the common priests too, but those of Aaron are somewhat more embellished. A special group of four other garments of simple linen was worn when acts of extraordinary holiness were performed. The four undergarments consisted of:

—A coat. Of Aaron's coat it is written: "You shall weave the coat in checkerwork of fine linen" (Exodus 28:39).

—A girdle. The girdle, bound around the coat, is also regarded as a vestment of distinction. Whereas the girdles of the common priests were made exclusively of fine twined linen (Exodus 28:39), Aaron's was of fine linen and dyed wools and was of embroidered work (Exodus 28:39).

—A headdress. For the common priests turbans or decorated turbans are prescribed, while Aaron wears a miter (Exodus 28:39–40). The decorated turban is considered an item of beauty and distinction, but more imposing is the miter, which is also used as a synonym for crown (Ezekiel 21:31).

—Breeches. The breeches are worn "to cover the flesh

of their nakedness, from the hips to the thighs" (Exodus 28:42).

The four outergarments that pertained specifically to the High Priest were of greater richness than the undergarments. They consisted of a mixture of dyed wool and fine linen. Some also contained threads of pure gold, while others were woven of golden filaments and yarn of a mixture of wool and linen. These costly substances indicated a high degree of holiness. The mixture of wool and linen was generally prohibited in profane garments, as it was associated with holiness. Precisely for this reason, however, it was preserved among the priests. In this respect, the priestly garments correspond to the curtains and veil of the Tabernacle, which are also said to have been made of a mixture of wool and linen, and to have displayed skillful workmanship.

The four outer garments had several features characteristic of royalty (the gold, the blue and the purple, as well as the crown), and when combined with the miter and with the anointing oil that was poured on the High Priest (Exodus 29:7), they gave him a sovereign appearance.

The four outer priestly garments are the ephod, the breastplate, the robe, and the plate (or crown).

—The ephod: Made of gold and a mixture of wool and linen (Exodus 18:6–12), it is the most distinguished of the priestly garments. The ephod served a unique purpose in early Israelite religion. The Israelite religion prohibited all soothsaying and divination by means of auguries, but did permit, side by side with prophecy, the priestly ephod. Both prophecy and the ephod were seen as means of seeking the counsel of God and of obtaining revelation of

His will. The ephod was engraved with the names of the Twelve Tribes (Exodus 28:9–12). The High Priest used the ephod along with the breastplate and the Urim and Thummim (see below) as a means of divination.

—The breastplate: The breastplate was attached to the ephod. In it were set twelve precious stones on which were engraved the tribes of Israel. On the breastplate rested the Urim and Thummim, a priestly device for obtaining oracles from God on behalf of the ruler (Numbers 27:21).

—The robe: The robe was worn under the ephod. It was made only of woolen threads, all of blue. On its hem hung bells of gold and pomegranates made of a mixture of dyed wool and fine linen (Exodus 28:31–35).

—The plate (Crown): It hung on a blue thread in front of the miter. Made of pure gold, it had two Hebrew words engraved on it meaning "Holy to God" (Exodus 28:36).

Commandments

According to rabbinic tradition, there are 613 command-ments (*Mitzvot* in Hebrew) in the Five Books of Moses. There are 365 negative commandments that tell us what we cannot do, and 248 positive ones that tell us what we should do. The list that follows was set forth by Maimonides in his **Book of Commandments**. The biblical sources are also cited.

MANDATORY COMMANDMENTS

God

The Jew is required to [1]believe that God exists and to [2]acknowledge His unity; to [3]love, [4]fear, and [5]serve Him. He is also commanded to [6]cleave to Him (by associating with and imitating the wise) and to [7]swear only by His name. One must [8]imitate God and [9]sanctify His name.

1. Ex. 20:22	5. Ex. 23:25	6. Deut. 10:20
2. Deut. 6:4	Deut. 11:13	7. Deut. 10:20
3. Deut. 6:5	(Deut. 6:13,	8. Deut. 28:9
4. Deut. 6:13	13:5)	9. Lev. 22:32

Torah

The Jew must [10]recite the *Shema* each morning and evening and [11]study the Torah and teach it to others. He should bind *tefillin* on his [12]head and [13]his arm. He should make [14]*zizit* for his garments and [15]fix a *mezuzah* on the door. The people are to be [16]assembled every seventh year to hear the Torah read and [17]the king must write a special copy of the Torah for himself. [18]Every Jew should have a Torah scroll. One should [19]praise God after eating.

10. Deut. 6:7	14. Num. 15:38	17. Deut. 17:18
11. Deut. 6:7	15. Deut. 6:9	18. Deut. 31:19
12. Deut. 6:8	16. Deut. 31:12	19. Deut. 8:10
13. Deut. 6:8		

Temple, and the Priests

The Jews should [20]build a Temple and [21]respect it. It must be [22]guarded at all times and the [23]Levites should perform their special duties in it. Before entering the Temple or participating in its service the priests [24]must wash their hands and feet; they must also [25]light the candelabrum daily. The priests are required to [26]bless Israel and to [27]set the shewbread and frankincense before the Ark. Twice daily they must [28]burn the incense on the golden altar. Fire shall be kept burning on the altar [29]continually and the ashes should be [30]removed daily. Ritually unclean persons must be [31]kept out of the Temple. Israel [32]should honor its priests, who must be [33]dressed in special priestly raiment. The priests should [34]carry the Ark on their shoulders, and the holy anointing oil [35]must be prepared according to its special formula. The priestly families should officiate in [36]rotation. In honor of certain dead close relatives the priests should [37]make themselves ritually unclean. The high priest may marry [38]only a virgin.

20. Ex. 25:8	27. Ex. 25:30	33. Ex. 28:2
21. Lev. 19:30	28. Ex. 30:7	34. Num. 7:9
22. Num. 18:4	29. Lev. 6:6	35. Ex. 30:31
23. Num. 18:23	30. Lev. 6:3	36. Deut. 18:6–8
24. Ex. 30:19	31. Num. 5:2	37. Lev. 21:2–3
25. Ex. 27:21	32. Lev. 21:8	38. Lev. 21:13
26. Num. 6:23		

Sacrifices

The [39]*tamid* sacrifice must be offered twice daily and the [40]high priest must also offer a meal-offering twice daily. An additional sacrifice (*musaf*) should be offered [41]every Sabbath, [42]on the first of every month, and [43]on each of the seven days of Passover. On the second day of Passover [44]a meal offering of the first barley must also be brought. On Shavuot a [45]*musaf* must be offered and [46]two loaves of bread as a wave offering. The additional sacrifice must also be made on [47]Rosh HaShanah and [48]on the Day of Atonement when the [49]Avodah must also be performed. On every day of the festival of [50]Sukkot a *musaf* must be brought as well as on the [51]eighth day thereof.

Every male Jew should make [52]pilgrimage to the Temple three times a year and [53]appear there during the three pilgrim Festivals. One should [54]rejoice on the Festivals.

On the 14th of Nisan one should [55]slaughter the paschal

lamb and [56]eat of its roasted flesh on the night of the 15th. Those who were ritually impure in Nisan should slaughter a paschal lamb on [57]the 14th of Iyyar and eat it with [58]*mazzah* and bitter herbs.

Trumpets should be [59]sounded when the festive sacrifices are brought and also in times of tribulation.

Cattle to be sacrificed must be [60]at least eight days old and [61]without blemish. All offerings must be [62]salted. It is a *mitzvah* to perform the ritual of [63]the burnt offering, [64]the sin offering, [65]the guilt offering, [66]the peace offering, and [67]the meal offering.

Should the Sanhedrin err in a decision its members [68]must bring a sin offering, which offering must also be brought [69]by a person who has unwittingly transgressed a *karet* prohibition (i.e., one that, if done deliberately, would incur *karet*). When one is in doubt as to whether one has transgressed such a prohibition, a [70]"suspensive" guilt offering must be brought. For [71]stealing or swearing falsely and for other sins of a like nature, a guilt offering must be brought. In special circumstances the sin offering [72]can be according to one's means.

One must [73]confess one's sins before God and repent for them. A [74]man or [75]a woman who has a seminal issue must bring a sacrifice; a woman must also bring a sacrifice [76]after childbirth. A leper must [77]bring a sacrifice after he has been cleansed.

One must [78]tithe one's cattle. The [79]firstborn of clean (i.e., permitted) cattle are holy and must be sacrificed. The firstborn of man must be [80]redeemed. The firstling of the ass must be [81]redeemed; if not [82]its neck has to be broken.

Animals set aside as offerings [83]must be brought to Jerusalem without delay and [84]may be sacrificed only in the

Temple. Offerings from outside the land of Israel [85]may also be brought to the Temple. Sanctified animals [86]which have become blemished must be redeemed. A beast exchanged for an offering [87]is also holy.

The priests should eat [88]the remainder of the meal offering and [89]the flesh of sin and guilt offerings; but consecrated flesh that has become [90]ritually unclean, or [91]that was not eaten within its appointed time must be burned.

39. Num. 28:3	58. Num. 9:11,	74. Lev. 15:13–15
40. Lev. 6:13	Ex. 12:8	75. Lev. 15:28–29
41. Num. 28:9	59. Num. 10:10,	76. Lev. 12:6
42. Num. 28:11	Num. 10:9	77. Lev. 14:10
43. Lev. 23:36	60. Lev. 22:27	78. Lev. 27:32
44. Lev. 23:10	61. Lev. 22:21	79. Ex. 13:2
45. Num. 28:26–27	62. Lev. 2:13	80. Ex. 22:28,
46. Lev. 23:17	63. Lev. 1:2	Num. 18:15
47. Num. 29:1–2	64. Lev. 6:18	81. Ex. 34:20
48. Num. 29:7–8	65. Lev. 7:1	82. Ex. 13:13
49. Lev. 16	66. Lev. 3:1	83. Deut. 12:5–5
50. Num. 29:13	67. Lev. 2:1, 6:7	84. Deut. 12:14
51. Num. 29:36	68. Lev. 4:13	85. Deut. 12:26
52. Ex. 23:14	69. Lev. 4:27	86. Deut. 12:15
53. Ex. 34:23,	70. Lev. 5:17–18	87. Lev. 27:33
Deut. 16:16	71. Lev. 5:15,	88. Lev. 6:9
54. Deut. 16:14	21–25,	89. Ex. 29:33
55. Ex. 12:6	19:20–21	90. Lev. 7:19
56. Ex. 12:8	72. Lev. 5:1–11	91. Lev. 7:17
57. Num. 9:11	73. Num. 5:6–7	

Vows

A Nazirite must [92]let his hair grow during the period of his separation. When that period is over he must [93]shave his head and bring his sacrifice.

A man must [94]honor his vows and his oaths, which a judge can [95]annul only in accordance with the law.

92. Num. 6:5   94. Deut.23:24   95. Num. 30:3
93. Num. 6:18

Ritual Purity

Anyone who touches [96]a carcass or [97]one of the eight species of reptiles becomes ritually unclean; food becomes unclean by [98]coming into contact with a ritually unclean object. Menstruous women [99]and those [100]lying-in after childbirth are ritually impure. A [101]leper, [102]a leprous garment, and [103]a leprous house are all ritually unclean. A man having [104]a running issue is unclean, as is [105]semen. A woman suffering from [106]running issue is also impure.

A [107]human corpse is ritually unclean. The purification water (*mei niddah*) purifies [108]the unclean, but it makes the clean ritually impure. It is a *mitzvah* to become ritually clean [109]by ritual immersion. To become cleansed of leprosy one [110]must follow the specified procedure and also [111]shave off all of one's hair. Until cleansed the leper [112]must be bareheaded with clothing in disarray so as to be easily distinguishable.

The ashes of [113]the red heifer are to be used in the process of ritual purification.

96. Lev. 11:8, 24	102. Lev. 13:51	108. Num. 19:13, 21
97. Lev. 11:29–31	103. Lev. 14:44	109. Lev. 15:16
98. Lev. 11:34	104. Lev. 15:2	110. Lev. 14:2
99. Lev. 15:19	105. Lev. 15:16	111. Lev. 14:9
100. Lev. 12:2	106. Lev. 15:19	112. Lev. 13:45
101. Lev. 13:3	107. Num. 19:14	113. Num. 19:2–9

Donations of the Temple

If a person [114]undertakes to give his own value to the Temple he must do so. Should a man declare [115]an unclean beast, [116]a house, or [117]a field as a donation to the Temple, he must give their value in money as fixed by the priest. If one unwittingly derives benefit from Temple property [118]full restitution plus a fifth must be made.

The fruit of [119]the fourth year's growth of trees is holy and may be eaten only in Jerusalem. When you reap your fields you must leave [120]the corners, [121]the gleanings, [122]the forgotten sheaves, [123]the misformed bunches of grapes and [124]the gleanings of the grapes for the poor.

The first fruits must be [125]separated and brought to the Temple and you must also [126]separate the great heave offering (*terumah*) and give it to the priests. You must give [127]one tithe of your produce to the Levites and separate [128]a second tithe which is to be eaten only in Jerusalem. The Levites [129]must give a tenth of their tithe to the priests.

In the third and sixth years of the seven-year cycle you should [130]separate a tithe for the poor instead of the second tithe. A declaration [131] must be recited when separating the various tithes and [132]when bringing the first fruits to the Temple.

The first portion of the [133]dough must be given to the priest.

114. Lev. 27:2–8
115. Lev. 27:11–12
116. Lev. 27:14
117. Lev. 27:16, 22–23
118. Lev. 5:16
119. Lev. 19:24
120. Lev. 19:9
121. Lev. 19:9
122. Deut. 24:19
123. Lev. 19:10
124. Lev. 19:10
125. Ex. 23:19
126. Deut. 18:4
127. Lev. 27:30, Num. 18:24
128. Deut. 14:22
129. Num. 18:26
130. Deut. 14:28
131. Deut. 26:13
132. Deut. 26:5
133. Num. 15:20

The Sabbatical Year

In the seventh year (*shemittah*) everything that grows is [134]ownerless and available to all; the fields [135]must lie fallow and you may not till the ground. You must [136]sanctify the Jubilee year (fiftieth) and on the Day of Atonement in that year [137]you must sound the *shofar* and set all Hebrew slaves free. In the Jubilee year all land is to be [138]returned to its ancestral owners and, generally, in a walled city [139]the seller has the right to buy back a house within a year of the sale.

Starting from entry into the land of Israel, the years of the Jubilee must be [140]counted and announced yearly and septennially.

In the seventh year [141]all debts are annulled but [142]one may exact a debt owned by a foreigner.

134. Ex. 23:11	137. Lev. 25:9	140. Lev. 25:8
135. Ex. 34:21	138. Lev. 25:24	141. Deut. 15:3
136. Lev. 25:10	139. Lev. 25:29–30	142. Deut. 15:3

Concerning Animals for Consumption

When you slaughter an animal you must [143]give the priest his share as you must also give him [144]the first of the fleece. When a man makes a *herem* (a special vow) you must [145]distinguish between that which belongs to the Temple (i.e., when God's name was mentioned in the vow) and between that which goes to the priests. To be fit for consumption, beast and fowl must be [146]slaughtered according to the law and if they are not of a domesticated species [147]their blood must be covered with earth after slaughter.

Set the parent bird [148]free when taking the nest. Examine

[149]beast, [150]fowl, [151]locusts, and [152]fish to determine whether they are permitted for consumption.

The Sanhedrin should [153]sanctify the first day of every month and reckon the years and the seasons.

143. Deut. 18:3	147. Lev. 17:13	151. Lev. 11:21
144. Deut. 18:4	148. Deut. 22:7	152. Lev. 11:9
145. Lev. 27:21, 28	149. Lev. 11:2	153. Ex. 12:2,
146. Deut. 12:21	150. Deut. 14:11	Deut. 16:1

Festivals

You must [154]rest on the Sabbath day and [155]declare it holy at its onset and termination. On the fourteenth of Nisan [156]remove all leaven from your ownership and on the night of the fifteenth [157]relate the story of the exodus from Egypt; on that night [158]you must also eat *mazzah*. On the [159]first and [160]seventh days of Passover you must rest. Starting from the day of the first sheaf (sixteenth of Nisan) you shall [161]count forty-nine days. You must rest on [162]Shavuot, and on [163]Rosh HaShanah; on the Day of Atonement you must [164]fast and [165]rest. You must also rest on [166]the first and [167]the eighth day of Sukkot, during which festival you shall [168]dwell in booths and [169]take the four species. On Rosh HaShanah [170]you are to hear the sound of the *shofar*.

154. Ex. 23:12	160. Ex. 12:16	166. Lev. 23:35
155. Ex. 20:8	161. Lev. 23:35	167. Lev. 23:36
156. Ex. 12:15	162. Lev. 23	168. Lev. 23:42
157. Ex. 13:8	163. Lev. 23:24	169. Lev. 23:40
158. Ex. 12:18	164. Lev. 16:29	170. Num. 29:1
159. Ex. 12:16	165. Lev. 16:29, 31	

Community

Every male should [171]give half a shekel to the Temple annually.

You must [172]obey a prophet and [173]appoint a king. You must also [174]obey the Sanhedrin; in the case of division, [175]yield to the majority. Judges and officials shall be [176]appointed in every town and they shall judge the people [177]impartially.

Whoever is aware of evidence [178]must come to court to testify. Witnesses shall be [179]examined thoroughly and, if found to be false, [180]shall have done to them what they intended to do to the accused.

When a person is found murdered and the murderer is unknown the ritual of [181]decapitating the heifer must be performed.

Six cities of refuge should be [182]established. The Levites, who have no ancestral share in the land, shall [183]be given cities to live in.

You must [184]build a fence around your roof and remove potential hazards from your home.

171. Ex. 30:12–13
172. Deut. 18:15
173. Deut. 17:15
174. Deut. 17:11
175. Ex. 23:2
176. Deut. 16:18
177. Lev. 19:15
178. Lev. 5:1
179. Deut. 13:15
180. Deut. 19:19
181. Deut. 21:4
182. Deut. 19:3
183. Num. 35:2
184. Deut. 22:8

Idolatry

Idolatry and its appurtenances [185]must be destroyed, and a city which has become perverted must be [186]treated according to the law. You are commanded to [187]destroy the seven Canaanite nations, and [188]to blot out the memory of Amalek, and [189]to remember what they did to Israel.

185. Deut. 12:2, 7:5   187. Deut. 20:17   189. Deut. 25:17
186. Deut. 13:17   188. Deut. 25:19

War

The regulations for wars other then those commanded in the Torah [190]are to be observed and a priest should be [191]appointed for special duties in times of war. The military camp must be [192]kept in a sanitary condition. To this end, every soldier must be [193]equipped with the necessary implements.

190. Deut. 20:11–12   192. Deut. 23:14–15   193. Deut. 23:14
191. Deut. 20:2

Social

Stolen property must be [194]restored to its owner. Give [195]charity to the poor. When a Hebrew slave goes free the owner must [196]give him gifts. Lend to [197]the poor without interest; to the foreigner you may [198]lend at interest. Restore [199]a pledge to its owner if he needs it. Pay the worker his wages [200]on time; [201]permit him to eat of the produce with which he is working. You must [202]help unload an animal when necessary, and also [203]help load man or beast. Lost property [204]must be restored to its owner. You are required [205]to reprove the sinner but you must [206]love your fellow as yourself. You are commanded [207]to love the proselyte. Your weights and measures [208]must be accurate.

194. Lev. 5:23	199. Deut. 24:13,	204. Deut. 22:1,
195. Deut. 15:8,	Ex. 22:25	Ex. 23:4
Lev. 25:35–36	200. Deut. 24:15	205. Lev. 19:17
196. Deut. 15:14	201. Deut. 23:25–26	206. Lev. 19:18
197. Ex. 22:24	202. Ex. 23:5	207. Deut. 10:19
198. Deut. 23:21	203. Deut. 22:4	208. Lev. 19:36

Family

Respect the [209]wise, [210]honor and [211] fear your parents. You should [212]perpetuate the human race by marrying [213]according to the law. A bridegroom is to [214]rejoice with his bride for one year. Male children must [215]be circumcised. Should a man die childless his brother must either [216]marry his widow or [217]release her (*halizah*). He who violates a virgin must [218]marry her and may never divorce her. If a man unjustly accuses his wife of premarital promiscuity [219]he shall be flogged, and may never divorce her. The seducer [220]must be punished according to the law. The female captive must be [221]treated in accordance with her special regulations. Divorce can be executed [222]only by means of written document. A woman suspected of adultery [223]has to submit to the required test.

209. Lev. 19:32	215. Gen. 17:10,	219. Deut. 22:18–19
210. Ex. 20:12	Lev. 12:3	220. Ex. 22:15–23
211. Lev. 19:3	216. Deut. 25:5	221. Deut. 21:11
212. Gen. 1:28	217. Deut. 25:9	222. Deut. 24:1
213. Deut. 24:1	218. Deut. 22:29	223. Num. 5:15–27
214. Deut. 24:5		

Judicial

When required by law [224]you must administer the punishment of flogging and you must [225]exile the unwitting homicide. Capital punishment shall be by [226]the sword, [227]strangulation, [228]fire, or [229]stoning, as specified. In some cases the body of the executed [230]shall be hanged, but it [231]must be brought to burial the same day.

224. Deut. 25:2	227. Lev. 21:16	230. Deut. 21:22
225. Num. 35:25	228. Lev. 20:14	231. Deut. 21:23
226. Ex. 21:20	229. Deut. 22:24	

Slaves

Hebrew slaves [232]must be treated according to the special laws for them. The master should [233]marry his Hebrew maidservant or [234]redeem her. The alien slave [235]must be treated according to the regulation applying to him.

232. Ex. 21:2	234. Ex. 21:8	235. Lev. 25:46
233. Ex. 21:8		

Torts

The applicable law must be administered in the case of injury caused by [236]a person, [237]an animal, or [238]a pit. Thieves [239]must be punished. You must render judgment in cases of [240]trespass by cattle, [241]arson, [242]embezzlement by an unpaid guardian, and in claims against [243]a paid guardian, a hirer, or [244]a borrower. Judgment must also be rendered in disputes arising out of [245]sales, [248]inheritance, and [246]other matters generally. You are required to [247]rescue the persecuted even if it means killing his oppressor.

236. Ex. 21:18	239. Ex. 21:37–22:3	242. Ex. 22:6–8
237. Ex. 21:28	240. Ex. 22:4	243. Ex. 22:9–12
238. Ex. 21:33–34	241. Ex. 22:5	244. Ex. 22:13

245. Lev. 25:14   247. Deut. 25:12   248. Num. 27:8
246. Ex. 22:8

PROHIBITIONS

Idolatry and Related Practices

It is [1]forbidden to believe in the existence of any but the One God.

You may not make images [2]for yourself or [3]for others to worship or for [4]any other purpose.

You must not worship anything but God either in [5]the manner prescribed for His or [6]in its own manner of worship.

Do not [7]sacrifice children to Molech.

You may not [8]practice necromancy or [9]resort to "familiar spirits," neither should you take idolatry or its mythology [10]seriously. It is forbidden to construct a [11]pillar or [12]dais even for the worship of God or to [13]plant trees in the Temple.

You may not [14]swear by idols or instigate an idolator to do so, nor may you encourage or persuade any [15]non-Jew or [16]Jew to worship idols.

You must not [17]listen to or love anyone who disseminates idolatry nor [18]should you withhold yourself from hating him. Do not [19]pity such a person. If somebody tries to convert you to idolatry [20]do not defend him or [21]conceal the fact.

It is forbidden to [22]derive any benefit from the ornaments of idols. You may not [23]rebuild that which has been destroyed as a punishment for idolatry nor may you [24]have any benefit from its wealth. Do not [25]use anything connected with idols or idolatry.

It is forbidden [26]to prophesy in the name of idols or

prophesy [27]falsely in the name of God. Do not [28]listen to the one who prophesies for idols and do not [29]fear the false prophet or hinder his execution.

You must not [30]imitate the ways of idolators or practice their customs. [31]Divination, [32]soothsaying, [33]enchanting, [34]sorcery, [35]charming, [36]consulting ghosts or [37]familiar spirits, and [38]necromancy are forbidden. Women must not [39]wear male clothing nor men [40]that of women. Do not [41]tattoo yourself in the manner of the idolators.

You may not wear [42]garments made of both wool and linen nor may you shave (with a razor) the sides of [43]your head or [44]your beard. Do not [45]lacerate yourself over your dead.

1. Ex. 20:3	18. Deut. 13:9	33. Deut. 18:10–11
2. Ex. 20:4	19. Deut. 13:9	Deut. 10:26
3. Lev. 19:4	20. Deut. 13:9	34. Deut. 18:10–11
4. Ex. 20:20	21. Deut. 13:9	35. Deut. 18:10–11
5. Ex. 20:5	22. Deut. 7:25	36. Deut. 18:10–11
6. Ex. 20:5	23. Deut. 13:17	37. Deut. 18:10–11
7. Lev. 18:21	24. Deut. 13:18	38. Deut. 18:10–11
8. Lev. 19:31	25. Deut. 7:26	39. Deut. 22:5
9. Lev. 19:31	26. Deut. 18:20	40. Deut. 22:5
10. Lev. 19:4	27. Deut. 18:20	41. Lev. 19:28
11. Deut. 16:22	28. Deut. 13:3, 4	42. Deut. 22:11
12. Lev. 20:1	Deut. 13:4	43. Lev. 19:27
13. Deut. 16:21	29. Deut. 18:22	44. Lev. 19:27
14. Ex. 23:13	30. Lev. 20:23	45. Deut. 16:1,
15. Ex. 23:13	31. Lev. 19:26	Deut. 14:1,
16. Deut. 13:12	Deut. 18:10	Lev. 19:28
17. Deut. 13:9	32. Deut. 18:10	

Prohibitions Resulting from Historical Events

It is forbidden to return to Egypt to [46]dwell there permanently or to [47]indulge in impure thoughts or sights. You may not [48]make a pact with the seven Canaanite nations or [49]save the life of any member of them. Do not [50]show mercy to idolators, [51]permit them to dwell in the land of Israel, or [52]intermarry with them. A Jewess may not [53]marry an Ammonite or Moabite even if he converts to Judaism but should not refuse (for reasons of genealogy alone) [54]a descendant of Esau or [55]an Egyptian who is a proselyte. It is prohibited to [56]make peace with the Ammonite or Moabite nations.

The [57]destruction of fruit trees even in times of war is forbidden, as is wanton waste at any time. Do not [58]fear the enemy and do not [59]forget the evil done by Amalek.

46. Deut. 17:16	50. Deut. 7:2	55. Deut. 23:8
47. Num. 15:39	51. Ex. 23:33	56. Deut. 23:7
48. Ex. 23:32,	52. Deut. 7:3	57. Deut. 20:19
Deut. 7:2	53. Deut. 23:4	58. Deut. 7:21
49. Deut. 20:16	54. Deut. 23:8	59. Deut. 25:19

Blasphemy

You must not [60]blaspheme the Holy Name, [61]break an oath made by It, [62]take It in vain or, [63]profane It. Do not [64]try the Lord God.

You may not [65]erase God's name from the holy texts or destroy institutions devoted to His worship. Do not [66]allow the body of one hanged to remain so overnight.

60. Lev. 24:16	62. Ex. 20:7	65. Deut. 12:4
rather Ex. 22:27	63. Lev. 22:32	66. Deut. 21:23
61. Lev. 19:12	64. Deut. 6:16	

Temple

Be not [67]lax in guarding the Temple.

The high priest must not enter the Temple [68]indiscriminately; a priest with a physical blemish may not [69]enter there at all or [70]serve in the sanctuary, and even if the blemish is of a temporary nature he may not [71]participate in the service until it has passed.

The Levites and the priests must not [72]interchange in their functions. Intoxicated persons may not [73]enter the sanctuary or teach the Law. It is forbidden for [74]non-priests, [75]unclean priests, or [76]priests who have performed the necessary ablution but are still within the time limit of their uncleanness to serve in the Temple. No unclean person may enter [77]the Temple or [78]the Temple Mount.

The altar must not be made of [79]hewn stones nor may the ascent to it be by [80]steps. The fire on it may not be [81]extinguished nor may any other but the specified incense be [82]burned on the golden altar. You may not [83]manufacture oil with the same ingredients and in the same proportions as the annointing oil, which itself [84]may not be misused. Neither may you [85]compound incense with the same ingredients and in the same proportions as that burnt on the altar. You must not [86]remove the staves from the Ark, [87]remove the breastplate from the ephod, or [88]make any incision in the upper garment of the high priest.

67. Num. 18:5
68. Lev. 16:2
69. Lev. 21:23
70. Lev. 21:17
71. Lev. 21:18
72. Num. 18:3
73. Lev. 10:9–11
74. Num. 18:4
75. Lev. 22:2
76. Lev. 21:6
77. Num. 5:3
78. Deut. 23:11
79. Ex. 20:25
80. Ex. 20:26
81. Lev. 6:6
82. Ex. 30:9
83. Ex. 30:32
84. Ex. 30:32
85. Ex. 30:37
86. Ex. 25:15
87. Ex. 28:28
88. Ex. 28:32

Sacrifices

It is forbidden to [89]offer sacrifices or [90]slaughter consecrated animals outside the Temple. You may not [91]sanctify, [92]slaughter, [93]sprinkle the blood of, or [94]burn the inner parts of a blemished animal even if the blemish is [95]of a temporary nature and even if it is [96]offered by Gentiles. It is forbidden to [97]inflict a blemish on an animal consecrated for sacrifice.

Leaven or honey may not [98]be offered on the altar, neither may [99]anything unsalted. An animal received as the hire of a harlot or as the price of a dog [100]may not be offered.

Do not [101]kill an animal and its young on the same day.

It is forbidden to use [102]olive oil or [103]frankincense in the sin offering or [104], [105], in the jealousy offering (*sotah*). You may not [106]substitute sacrifices even [107]from one category to the other. You may not [108]redeem the firstborn of permitted animals. It is forbidden to [109]sell the tithe of the herd or [110]sell or [111]redeem a field consecrated by the *herem* vow.

When you slaughter a bird for a sin offering you may not [112]split its head.

It is forbidden to [113]work with or [114]to shear a consecrated animal. You must not slaughter the paschal lamb [115]while there is still leaven about; nor may you leave overnight [116]those parts that are to be offered up or [117]to be eaten. You may not leave any part of the festive offering [118]until the third day or any part of [119]the second paschal lamb or [120]the thanksgiving offering until the morning.

It is forbidden to break a bone of [121]the first or [122]the second paschal lamb or [123]to carry their flesh out of the house where it is being eaten. You must not [124]allow the remains of the meal offering to become leaven. It is also forbidden to eat the paschal lamb [125]raw or sodden or to allow [126]an alien resident, [127]an uncircumcised person, or an [128]apostate to eat of it.

A ritually unclean person [129]must not eat of holy things nor may [130]holy things which have become unclean be eaten. Sacrificial meat [131]which is left after the time-limit or [132]which was slaughtered with wrong intentions must not be eaten. The heave offering must not be eaten by [133]a non-priest, [134]a priest's sojourner or hired worker, [135]an uncircumcised person, or [136]an unclean priest. The daughter of a priest who is married to a non-priest may not [137]eat of holy things. The meal offering of the priest [138]must not be eaten, neither may [139]the flesh of the sin offerings sacrificed within the sanctuary or [140]consecrated animals which have become blemished.

You may not eat the second tithe of [141]corn, [142]wine, or [143]oil, or [144]unblemished firstlings outside Jerusalem. The priests may not eat the [145]sin-offerings, or the trespass-offerings outside the temple courts or [146]the flesh of the burnt-offering at all. The lighter sacrifices [147]may not be eaten before the blood has been sprinkled. A non-priest may not [148]eat of the holiest sacrifices, and a priest [149]may not eat the first-fruits outside the Temple courts.

One may not eat [150]the second tithe while in a state of impurity or [151]in mourning; its redemption money [152]may not be used for anything other than food and drink.

You must not [153]eat untithed produce or [154]change the order of separating the various tithes.

Do not [155]delay payment of offerings—either freewill or obligatory—and do not [156]come to the Temple on the pilgrim festivals without an offering.

Do not [157]break your word.

89. Deut. 12:13
90. Lev. 17:3-4
91. Lev. 22:20
92. Lev. 22:22
93. Lev. 22:24
94. Lev. 22:22
95. Deut. 17:1
96. Lev. 22:25
97. Lev. 22:21
98. Lev. 2:11
99. Lev. 2:13
100. Deut. 23:19
101. Lev. 22:28
102. Lev. 5:11
103. Lev. 5:11
104. Num. 5:15
105. Num. 5:15
106. Lev. 27:10
107. Lev. 27:26
108. Num. 18:17
109. Lev. 27:33
110. Lev. 27:28
111. Lev. 27:28

112. Lev. 5:8
113. Deut. 15:19
114. Deut. 15:19
115. Ex. 34:25
116. Ex. 23:10
117. Ex. 12:10
118. Deut. 16:4
119. Num. 9:13
120. Lev. 22:30
121. Ex. 12:46
122. Num. 9:12
123. Ex. 12:46
124. Lev. 6:10
125. Ex. 12:9
126. Ex. 12:45
127. Ex. 12:48
128. Ex. 12:43
129. Lev. 12:4
130. Lev. 7:19
131. Lev. 19:6-8
132. Lev. 7:18
133. Lev. 22:10
134. Lev. 22:10

135. Lev. 22:10
136. Lev. 22:4
137. Lev. 22:12
138. Lev. 6:16
139. Lev. 6:23
140. Deut. 14:3
141. Deut. 12:17
142. Deut. 12:17
143. Deut. 12:17
144. Deut. 12:17
145. Deut. 12:17
146. Deut. 12:17
147. Deut. 12:17
148. Deut. 12:17
149. Ex. 29:33
150. Deut. 26:14
151. Deut. 26:14
152. Deut. 26:14
153. Lev. 22:15
154. Ex. 22:28
155. Deut. 23:22
156. Ex. 23:15
157. Num. 30:3

Priests

A priest may not marry [158]a harlot, [159]a woman who has been profaned from the priesthood, or [160]a divorcee; the high priest must not [161]marry a widow or [162]take one as a concubine. Priests may not enter the sanctuary with [163]overgrown hair of the head or [164]with torn clothing; they must not [165]leave the courtyard during the Temple service. An ordinary priest may not render himself [166]ritually impure except for those relatives specified, and the high priest should not become impure [167]for anybody in [168]any way.

The tribe of Levi shall have no part in [169]the division of the land of Israel or [170]in the spoils of war.

It is forbidden [171]to make oneself bald as a sign of mourning for one's dead.

158. Lev. 21:7	163. Lev. 10:6	168. Lev. 21:11
159. Lev. 21:7	164. Lev. 10:6	169. Deut. 18:1
160. Lev. 21:7	165. Lev. 10:7	170. Deut. 18:1
161. Lev. 21:14	166. Lev. 21:1	171. Deut. 14:1
162. Lev. 21:15	167. Lev. 21:11	

Dietary Laws

A Jew may not eat [172]unclean cattle, [173]unclean fish, [174]unclean fowl, [175]creeping things that fly, [176]creatures that creep on the ground, [177]reptiles, [178]worms found in fruit or produce, or [179]any detestable creature.

An animal that has died naturally [180]is forbidden for consumption, as is [181]a torn or mauled animal. One must not eat [182]any limb taken from a living animal. Also prohibited is [183]the sinew of the thigh (*gid ha-nasheh*), as are [184]blood and [185]certain types of fat (*helev*). It is forbidden [186]to cook meat together with milk or [187]eat of such a mixture. It is also forbidden to eat [188]of an ox condemned to stoning (even should it have been properly slaughtered).

One may not eat [189]bread made of new corn or the new corn itself, either [190]roasted or [191]green, before the *omer* offering has been brought on the sixteenth of Nisan. You may not eat [192]*orlah* or [193]the growth of mixed planting in the vineyard. Any use of [194]wine libations to idols is prohibited, as are [195]gluttony and drunkenness. One may not eat anything on [196]the Day of Atonement. During Passover it is forbidden to eat [197]leaven (*hamez*) or [198]anything

containing an admixture of such. This is also forbidden
[199]after the middle of the fourteenth of Nisan (the day
before Passover). During Passover no leaven may be
[200]seen or [201]found in your possession.

172. Deut. 14:7	183. Gen. 32:33	193. Deut. 22:9
173. Lev. 11:11	184. Lev. 7:26	194. Deut. 32:38
174. Lev. 11:13	185. Lev. 7:23	195. Lev. 19:26,
175. Deut. 14:19	186. Ex. 23:19	Deut. 21:20
176. Lev. 11:41	187. Ex. 34:26	196. Lev. 23:29
177. Lev. 11:44	188. Ex. 21:28	197. Ex. 13:3
178. Lev. 11:42	189. Lev. 23:14	198. Ex. 13:20
179. Lev. 11:43	190. Lev. 23:14	199. Deut. 16:3
180. Deut. 14:21	191. Lev. 23:14	200. Ex. 13:7
181. Ex. 22:30	192. Lev. 19:23	201. Ex. 12:19
182. Deut. 12:23		

Nazirites

A Nazirite may not drink [202]wine or any beverage made
from grapes; he may not eat [203]fresh grapes, [204]dried grapes,
[205]grape seeds, or [206]grape peel. He may not render himself
[207]ritually impure for his dead nor may he [208]enter a tent in
which there is a corpse. He must not [209]shave his hair.

202. Num. 6:3	205. Num. 6:4	208. Lev. 21:11
203. Num. 6:3	206. Num. 6:4	209. Num. 6:5
204. Num. 6:3	207. Num. 6:7	

Agriculture

It is forbidden [210]to reap the whole of a field without leaving
the corners for the poor; it is also forbidden to [211]gather up
the ears of corn that fall during reaping, or to harvest [212]the
misformed clusters of grapes, or [213]the grapes that fall, or to
[214]return to take a forgotten sheaf.

You must not [215]sow different species of seed together or [216]corn in a vineyard; it is also forbidden to [217]crossbreed different species of animals or [218]work with two different species yoked together.

You must not [219]muzzle an animal working in a field to prevent it from eating.

It is forbidden to [220]till the earth, [221]to prune trees, [222]to reap (in the usual manner) produce or [223]fruit which has grown without cultivation in the seventh year (*shemittah*). One may also not [224]till the earth or prune trees in the Jubilee year, when it is also forbidden to harvest (in the usual manner) [225]produce or [226]fruit that has grown without cultivation.

One may not [227]sell one's landed inheritance in the land of Israel permanently or [228]change the lands of the Levites or [229]leave the Levites without support.

210. Lev. 23:22
211. Lev. 19:9
212. Lev. 19:10
213. Lev. 19:10
214. Deut. 24:19
215. Lev. 19:19
216. Deut. 22:9
217. Lev. 19:19
218. Deut. 22:10
219. Deut. 25:4
220. Lev. 25:4
221. Lev. 25:4
222. Lev. 25:5
223. Lev. 25:5
224. Lev. 25:11
225. Lev. 25:11
226. Lev. 25:11
227. Lev. 25:23
228. Lev. 25:33
229. Deut. 12:19

Loans, Business, and the Treatment of Slaves

It is forbidden to [230]demand repayment of a loan after the seventh year; you may not, however, [231]refuse to lend to the poor because that year is approaching. Do not [232]deny charity to the poor or [233]send a Hebrew slave away empty-handed when he finishes his period of service. Do not [234]dun your debtor when you know that he cannot pay.

It is forbidden to [235]lend to or [236]borrow from another Jew at interest or [237]participate in an agreement involving interest either as a guarantor, witness, or writer of the contract. Do not [238]delay payment of wages.

You may not [239]take a pledge from a debtor by violence, [240]keep a poor man's pledge when he needs it, or [241]take any pledge from a widow or [242]from any debtor if he earns his living with it.

Kidnaping [243]a Jew is forbidden.

Do not [244]steal or [245]rob by violence. Do not [246]remove a landmarker or [247]defraud.

It is forbidden [248]to deny receipt of a loan or a deposit or [249]to swear falsely regarding another man's property.

You must not [250]deceive anybody in business. You may not [251]mislead a man even verbally. It is forbidden to harm the stranger among you [252]verbally or [253]do him injury in trade. You may not [254]return or [255]otherwise take advantage of a slave who has fled to the land of Israel from his master, even if his master is a Jew.

Do not [256]afflict the widow or the orphan. You may not [257]misuse or [258]sell a Hebrew slave; do not [259]treat him cruelly or [260]allow a heathen to mistreat him. You must not [261]sell your Hebrew maidservant or, if you marry her, [262]withhold food, clothing, and conjugal rights from her. You must not [263]sell a female captive or [264]treat her as a slave.

Do not [265]covet another man's possessions even if you are willing to pay for them. Even [266]the desire alone is forbidden.

A worker must not [267]cut down standing corn during his work or [268]take more fruit than he can eat.

One must not [269]turn away from a lost article which is to

be returned to its owner, nor may you [270]refuse to help a man or an animal that is collapsing under its burden.

It is forbidden to [271]defraud with weights and measures or even [272]to possess inaccurate weights.

230. Deut. 15:2	245. Lev. 19:13	259. Lev. 25:43
231. Deut. 15:9	246. Deut. 19:14	260. Lev. 25:53
232. Deut. 15:7	247. Lev. 19:13	261. Ex. 21:8
233. Deut. 15:13	248. Lev. 19:11	262. Ex. 21:10
234. Ex. 22:24	249. Lev. 19:11	263. Deut. 21:14
235. Lev. 25:37	250. Lev. 25:14	264. Deut. 21:14
236. Deut. 23:20	251. Lev. 25:17	265. Ex. 20:17
237. Ex. 22:24	252. Ex. 22:20	266. Deut. 5:18
238. Lev. 19:13	253. Ex. 22:20	267. Deut. 23:26
239. Deut. 24:10	254. Deut. 23:16	268. Deut. 23:25
240. Deut. 24:12	255. Deut. 23:17	269. Deut. 22:3
241. Deut. 24:17	256. Ex. 22:21	270. Ex. 23:5
242. Deut. 24:6	257. Lev. 25:39	271. Lev. 19:35
243. Ex. 20:13	258. Lev. 25:42	272. Deut. 25:13
244. Lev. 19:11		

Justice

A judge must not [273]perpetuate injustice, [274]accept bribes, or be [275]partial or [276]afraid. He may [277]not favor the poor or [278]discriminate against the wicked; he should not [279]pity the condemned or [280]pervert the judgment of strangers or orphans.

It is forbidden to [281]hear one litigant without the other being present. A capital case cannot be decided by [282]a majority of one.

A judge should not [283]accept a colleague's opinion unless he is convinced of its correctness; it is forbidden to [284]appoint as a judge someone who is ignorant of the law.

Do not [285]give false testimony or accept [286]testimony

from a wicked person or from [287]relatives of a person involved in the case. It is forbidden to pronounce judgment [288]on the basis of the testimony of one witness.

Do not [289]murder.

You must not convict on [290]circumstantial evidence alone.

A witness [291]must not sit as a judge in capital cases.

You must not [292]execute anybody without due proper trial and conviction.

Do not [293]pity or spare the pursuer.

Punishment is not to be inflicted for [294]an act committed under duress.

Do not accept ransom [295]for a murderer or [296]a manslayer.

Do not [297]hesitate to save another person from danger and do not [298]leave a stumbling block in the way or [299]mislead another person by giving wrong advice.

It is forbidden [300]to administer more than the assigned number of lashes to the guilty.

Do not [301]tell tales or [302]bear hatred in your heart. It is forbidden to [303]shame a Jew, [304]to bear a grudge, or [305]to take revenge.

Do not [306]take the dam when you take the young birds.

It is forbidden to [307]shave a leprous scall or [308]remove other signs of that affliction. It is forbidden [309]to cultivate a valley in which a slain body was found and in which subsequently the ritual of breaking the heifer's neck (*eglah arufah*) was performed.

Do not [310]suffer a witch to live.

Do not [311]force a bridegroom to perform military service during the first year of his marriage. It is forbidden to [312]rebel against the transmitters of the tradition or to [313]add or [314]detract from the precepts of the law.

Do not curse [315]a judge, [316]a ruler, or [317]any Jew.

Do not [318]curse or [319]strike a parent.

It is forbidden to [320]work on the Sabbath or [321]walk further than the permitted limits (*eruv*). You may not [322]inflict punishment on the Sabbath.

It is forbidden to work on [323]the first or [324]the seventh day of Passover, on [325]Shavuot, on [326]Rosh HaShanah, on the [327]first and [328]eighth (*Shemini Azeret*) days of Sukkot, and [329]on the Day of Atonement.

273. Lev. 19:15	292. Num. 35:12	312. Deut. 17:11
274. Ex. 23:8	293. Deut. 25:12	313. Deut. 13:1
275. Lev. 19:15	294. Deut. 22:26	314. Deut. 13:1
276. Deut. 1:17	295. Num. 35:31	315. Ex. 22:27
277. Lev. 19:15,	296. Num. 35:32	316. Ex. 22:27
rather Ex. 23:3	297. Lev. 19:16	317. Lev. 19:14
278. Ex. 23:6	298. Deut. 22:8	318. Ex. 21:17
279. Deut. 19:13	299. Lev. 19:14	319. Ex. 21:15
280. Deut. 24:17	300. Deut. 25:23	320. Ex. 20:10
281. Ex. 23:1	301. Lev. 19:16	321. Ex. 16:29
282. Ex. 23:2	302. Lev. 19:17	322. Ex. 35:3
283. Ex. 23:2	303. Lev. 19:17	323. Ex. 12:16
284. Deut. 1:17	304. Lev. 19:18	324. Ex. 12:16
285. Ex. 20:16	305. Lev. 19:18	325. Lev. 23:21
286. Ex. 23:1	306. Deut. 22:6	326. Lev. 23:25
287. Deut. 24:16	307. Lev. 13:33	327. Lev. 23:35
288. Deut. 19:15	308. Duet. 24:8	328. Lev. 23:36
289. Ex. 20:13	309. Deut. 21:4	329. Lev. 23:28
290. Ex. 23:7	310. Ex. 22:17	
291. Num. 35:30	311. Deut. 24:5	

Incest and Other Forbidden Relationships

It is forbidden to enter into an incestuous relationship with one's [330]mother, [331]step-mother, [332]sister, [333]half-sister, [334]son's daughter, [335]daughter's daughter, [336]daughter, [337]any woman and her daughter, [338]any woman and her son's daughter, [339]any woman and her daughter's daughter, [340]father's sister, [341]mother's sister, [342]paternal uncle's wife, [343]daughter-in-law, [344]brother's wife, and [345]wife's sister.

It is also forbidden to [346]have sexual relations with a menstruous woman.

Do not [347]commit adultery.

It is forbidden for [348]a man or [349]a woman to have sexual intercourse with an animal.

Homosexuality [350]is forbidden, particularly with [351]one's father or [352]uncle.

It is forbidden to have [353]intimate physical contact (even without actual intercourse) with any of the women with whom intercourse is forbidden.

A *mamzer* may not [354]marry a Jewess.

Harlotry [355]is forbidden.

A divorcee may not be [356]remarried to her first husband if in the meanwhile she had married another.

A childless widow may not [357]marry anybody other than her late husband's brother.

A man may not [358]divorce a wife whom he married after have raped her or [359]after having slandered her.

An eunuch may not [360]marry a Jewess.

Castration [361]is forbidden.

330. Lev. 18:7	341. Lev. 18:13	352. Lev. 18:14
331. Lev. 18:8	342. Lev. 18:14	353. Lev. 18:6
332. Lev. 18:9	343. Lev. 18:15	354. Deut. 23:3
333. Lev. 18:11	344. Lev. 18:16	355. Deut. 23:18
334. Lev. 18:10	345. Lev. 18:18	356. Deut. 24:4
335. Lev. 18:10	346. Lev. 18:19	357. Deut. 25:5
336. Lev. 18:10	347. Lev. 18:20	358. Deut. 22:29
337. Lev. 18:17	348. Lev. 18:23	359. Deut. 22:19
338. Lev. 18:17	349. Lev. 18:23	360. Deut. 23:2
339. Lev. 18:17	350. Lev. 18:22	361. Lev. 22:24
340. Lev. 18:12	351. Lev. 18:7	

The Monarchy

You may not [362]elect as king anybody who is not of the seed of Israel.

The king must not accumulate an excessive number of [363]horses or [364]wives, or excessive [365]wealth.

362. Deut. 17:15   364. Deut. 17:17   365. Deut. 17:17
363. Deut. 17:16

Key to Abbreviations: Ex.—Exodus, Deut.—Deuteronomy, Lev.—Leviticus, Num.—Numbers, Gen.—Genesis.

Covenants

A covenant is a general obligation between two parties. It was confirmed in biblical times by an oath, a solemn meal, or sacrifices, or by some other dramatic act such as dividing an animal and passing the portions between the parties. In the Bible, the covenant par excellence is that between God and Israel. Following are eight examples of covenants in the Bible.

1. Noah's covenant with God: The sign of this covenant was the rainbow, which God said would be His promise that the earth would never again be destroyed by a flood (Genesis 8:21–22).
2. God's covenant with Abraham: Abraham is told by God to leave his homeland of Mesopotamia and go to a land that will be shown to him. There God says that He will make of Abraham a great nation (Genesis 12:1–3).
3. God's covenant with Moses and Israel: Moses is told that if the Israelites listen to God's voice and keep His covenant, then they will be God's own treasure from among all peoples (Exodus 19:5).

4. Moses calls the people of Israel together to renew the covenant: Here, all the people of Israel are called together to reenter into God's covenant. Even people who are not physically present at this large meeting of people are told that they too have automatically become a part of this covenant (Deuteronomy 29:9–14).

5. Joshua's renewal of the covenant: By the time Joshua nears death, it has apparently come to be taken for granted that the land belongs to the people of Israel. Therefore, as his final act of leadership, Joshua renews the covenant before returning the listeners each to his possession of land (Joshua 24:1–28).

6. Jehoida the priest solemnizes the covenant between God and the people: In this mediated covenant of renewal, all the people of Israel go to the temple of Baal and tear it to pieces (II Kings 11:17–20).

7. Josiah reads the covenantal scroll: In this religious renewal, King Josiah solemnizes the covenant before God, promising that the people will follow God and observe His commandments (II Kings 13:1–4).

8. Ezra renews the covenant: Here, Ezra brings the Torah scroll and reads it, explaining it to the people living in the land of Israel (Nehemiah 10:1).

Dietary Laws

One of the distinguishing features of Judaism is the observance of the dietary laws, which specify what foods are ritually clean or unclean and so may or may not be eaten. Although these restraining laws may have had their origin in ancient taboos or folk belief, they served to set the Jewish people apart from others. Following is a summary of the dietary laws.

REASON FOR KEEPING THE DIETARY LAWS

The Bible gives the reason for the dietary laws as a religious injunction imposed on the Israelites, based on the concept of holiness. Israel was commanded by God to take on the obligation of a sanctified people, apart from the pagan world:

> I am the Lord your God who has set you apart from the nations. You shall, therefore, separate between the clean beast and the

unclean, between the unclean fowl and the clean. You shall not make your souls detestable by beast or by fowl or by anything with which the ground teems, which I have set apart for you to hold unclean. You shall be holy unto Me, for I the Lord am holy and have set you apart from the peoples, that you should be Mine. (Leviticus 20:24–27)

PERMITTED AND FORBIDDEN FOOD

1. Animals: The general rule applying to animals is "whatsoever parts the hoof and is cloven footed, and chews the cud, that you may eat" (Leviticus 11:3). Forbidden foods include the camel, hare, rock badger, coney, and swine. Acceptable foods include the ox, sheep, goat, hart, roebuck, fallow-deer, wild goat, antelope and chamois.

2. Birds: In general, all birds of prey and birds seizing food with their claws and lifting it up before eating it are considered unclean and prohibited. Permitted fowl include those with projecting claws (one longer than the other), a crop, and a stomach the membrane of which is easily peeled off (Leviticus 11:13–19).

Forbidden birds include the eagle, ossifrage, ospray, vulture, kite, raven, owl, night hawk, cuckoo, cormorant, swan, pelican, stork, heron, bat, and all fowl that creep on all fours.

Acceptable fowl include the goose, chicken, dove, quail, sparrow, duck, and turkey.

3. Fish: The Bible does not mention the specific fish that are prohibited or acceptable. It indicates only how they may be recognized (Leviticus 11:9–12).

Forbidden fish are those having no fins or scales in the water. Included in this category would be eel and all shellfish such as oysters, lobsters, and the like.

Acceptable fish are those that have fins and scales. Included in this category are the salmon, perch, pike, trout, bass, tuna, and the like.

4. Winged Animals: Reference here is made to insects that multiply rapidly and become pests to humans (Leviticus 11:20–23).

Forbidden ones are all winged swarming things that creep and go about upon all four legs.

Acceptable: The Bible mentions several types of locusts that are permitted, but tradition forbids every species of winged insects.

5. Creeping Things: The general rule is that every creature that creeps on earth is forbidden to be eaten (Leviticus 11:29–43). This would include worms, snakes, snails, crabs, lizards, and the like.

6. Products of Forbidden Foods: Anything that is derived from forbidden foods is also prohibited from being eaten. This would apply to milk from unclean animals, eggs from forbidden fowl, and roe from forbidden fish.

7. Fats: The fat of an ox, sheep, or goat (sacrificial animals) is forbidden (Leviticus 7:23), as is the abdominal fat of clean animals. This rule applies only to certain parts of the above animals that were designated for sacrificial purposes in Bible times. All other fats of the animal may be eaten. The fats of birds or permitted wild animals are likewise permitted for us.

8. Sinews and Hindquarters: In the story of Jacob wrestling with an angel it is told that Jacob was rendered lame in the struggle: "Therefore the children of Israel do

not eat of the sinew which shrank, which is upon the hollow thigh until this day, because the angel touched the hollow of Jacob's thigh in the sinew that shrank" (Genesis 32:33). In conformity with tradition, the hindquarters of cattle are prohibited because of the difficulty in the removal of the veins from this part of the animal.

9. Forbidden Use of Blood: "No soul of you shall eat blood, neither shall any stranger that sojourns among you eat blood" (Leviticus 17:12). Blood is supposed to contain the vital element of life. Therefore, the blood of beasts and fowl must be removed before they may be eaten.

Dreams

The biblical view of dreams agrees substantially with that held by almost all ancient peoples. Dreams are visions of things actually transpiring on an ultramundane plane, where persons are not bound to bodies nor events to specific moments and places. This plane is indistinguishable from that of the gods (or God), and dreams are therefore considered to be divine communications. Following are some examples of biblical dreams.

1. The first dream: The first recorded dream in the Bible is an appearance of God to Avimelech, who is living with Sarah, Abraham's wife, to tell him to return Sarah to Abraham. As a reward for heeding the dream and restoring Sarah to Abraham, Avimelech acquires a large family (Genesis 20).
2. Jacob's dream of the heavenly ladder: In this dream, Jacob dreams of a ladder that reaches from the earth to the heavens, with angels ascending and descending upon it (Genesis 28:21).
3. Joseph's dreams: In one of Joseph's two early

dreams, a series of sheaves are bowing down to one sheaf. In another, the sun and moon and eleven stars bow down to Joseph. Both of these dreams, interpreted as Joseph's superiority to his brothers, antagonize the brothers and lead to the sale of Joseph to the Midianite caravan (Genesis 37:6–8, 9–11).

4. Pharaoh's dreams: In two dreams of Pharaoh, seven lean cows devour seven fat cows, and seven thin ears of corn swallow up seven thick ears of corn. Joseph interprets these dreams as forecasting a seven year famine in Egypt as well as seven years of plenty. For his correct interpretation, Joseph is elevated to a position of royalty in Pharaoh's Egyptian house (Genesis 41:1–7, 25–32).

5. The Tent Dream: Despite all the Bible's cautions about false dreams, quite a few kings, prophets, and citizens of the realm received significant dreams. The victory over the Midianites is foreseen in a strange dream that comes to one of Gideon's soldiers: "there was a man that told a dream to his fellow, and said, Behold, I dreamed a dream, and a cake of barley bread tumbled into the host of Midian, and came to a tent, and smote it that it fell, and overturned it, that the tent lay along" (Judges 7:13).

6. Solomon's Dream: Soon after taking the throne, King Solomon has a dream in which God appears to him, asking what he should be given. Solomon asks for a discerning heart to judge the people (I Kings 3:5–10).

7. Nebuchadnezzar's Statue Dream: The dream that troubled King Nebuchadnezzar is one of the strangest in the Bible. The king saw the image of a man who had a head of gold, an upper torso of silver, and a lower torso of brass. "His legs were of iron, his feet part of iron and part clay." The statue was broken to pieces by a stone "cut out without hands," and like "the chaff of the

summer threshing floors" the pieces were carried away by the wind. The stone that destroyed the image became a great mountain that "filled the whole earth" (Daniel 2:31–35) Daniel interprets this dream, explaining to the king that the head of gold was the king, a lesser king following King Nebuchadnezzar was the silver, followed by one who would rule everywhere (brass) and one of great strength (iron). Daniel is rewarded for his analysis by being promoted to chief of the governors.

8. Daniel's Dream: In Daniel's dream he saw four wondrous beasts rise out of the sea. "The first beast was like a lion, and had eagle's wings (Daniel 7:4–7). The second beast was like a bear, the third like a leopard, and the fourth had iron teeth." It was thought that the first beast was King Nebuchadnezzar, the second the coalition of the Persians and Medes, the third Alexander the Great and the fourth the Roman Empire.

Earthquakes

It is conjectured that a number of earthquakes took place during biblical times. Following is a listing of some of the more memorable ones.

1. The earthquake at Sodom and Gomorrah (Genesis 19:24–25).
2. When Moses assembled the Israelites at the foot of Mount Sinai, the mountain smoked like a furnace and "quaked greatly" (Exodus 19:17–18).
3. During the rebellion of Korach, 250 people were swallowed up when "the ground clave asunder" (Numbers 16:31–33).
4. During King Saul's reign, when Jonathan attacked the Philistine garrison at Michmash, "the earth quaked" and there was great trembling (I Samuel 14:15).
5. During the reign of Ahab, the prophet Elijah fled because Jezebel had threatened to kill him. Elijah took shelter in a cave near Mount Sinai. Later, when he told God that the Israelites had forsaken the covenant and only he was still faithful, "a great and strong wind rent the

mountains, breaking the pieces into rocks, and after the wind an earthquake" (I Kings 19:9–12).

6. An earthquake during King Uzziah's rule was so severe that people fled (Zechariah 14:5).

7. Deborah's song makes reference to an earthquake when she sings, "O God, when you came forth from Seir . . . the earth trembled . . . the mountains quaked" (Judges 5:2–5).

English Words of Biblical Hebrew Origin

A fairly large number of Hebrew Bible words have passed directly into the English language, mostly in a religious context. The following is a partial list of some of the more well-known ones:

1. **Amen.** "So be it."

2. **Baal.** Name of a Phoenician god, and hence today of any idol.

3. **Bedlam.** A corruption of Bethlehem, deriving from the notorious insane asylum of St. Mary of Bethlehem. Today by extension "bedlam" has come to mean confusion.

4. **Behemoth.** Plural of *behemah*, "beast." Perhaps applied to the hippopotamus but signifying any huge creature.

5. **Camel.** From the Hebrew *gamal*.

6. **Cherub**. An angelic being, later interpreted to mean a beautiful and innocent child.

7. **Ephod**. A priestly vestment.

8. **Gehenna**. Meaning "hell," it derives from the Hebrew *Gei Hinnom*—the Valley of Hinnom, a place near ancient Jerusalem that was disfigured by human sacrifice and idolatrous rites.

9. **Halleluyah**. Praise God.

10. **Ichabod**. The glory has departed.

11. **Jubilee**. From Hebrew *yovel*, meaning twelve months of emancipation and restoration observed every fifty years and proclaimed by a *yovel* or ram's horn. Today the jubilee refers to any fiftieth anniversary or joyous season.

12. **Leviathan**. A sea monster or whale.

13. **Manna**. Food that God provided for the Israelites in the wilderness, and hence any sweet and refreshing substance.

14. **Messiah**. The "anointed one," or promised deliverer.

15. **Myrrh**. From the Hebrew *mor*, meaning spice.

16. **Paschal**. Relating to the Jewish Passover or to Easter.

17. **Sabbath**. The seventh day, a day of rest.

18. **Satan**. "Adversary," a name for the Devil.

19. **Selah**. Likely a musical direction.

20. **Seraph**. A celestial being.

21. **Shibboleth**. A flowing stream in the Bible. Today it has come to mean any catchword or slogan indicating a sect or party.

Escapes

The Bible is filled with adventure and intrigue. The following is a partial listing of great escapes in the Bible:

1. Lot and his two daughters escaped the destruction of Sodom (Genesis 19:15–26).

2. The ten plagues allowed 600,000 Israelites to escape Egypt (Exodus 12:37).

3. Two spies who went to Jericho escaped because Rachab hid them on her roof (Joshua 2:1–22).

4. Samson escaped the Philistines by breaking new ropes that bound him. He then found the jawbone of an ass and killed one thousand men (Judges 15:11–15).

5. While David was fleeing from Saul, his wife let him down through a window and put an idol in his bed to fool Saul's messengers (I Samuel 19:12–16).

6. David escaped the King of Gat by pretending to be a madman (I Samuel 21:10–22:1).

7. Jonathan and Achimaaz escaped from Absalom's men by hiding in a well that a woman covered to look like a pile of grain (II Samuel 17:15–21).

8. Jonah tried to flee to Tarshish from God's presence (Jonah 1:3).

Families with
the Most Children

Unlike families of modern times, biblical families tended to be quite large. Here is a partial listing of some of the largest families in biblical times:

1. Abdon had forty sons and thirty nephews (Judges 12:13, 14).

2. Abijah had twenty-two sons and sixteen daughters (II Chronicles 13:21).

3. Ahab had seventy sons (II Kings 10:1).

4. David had nineteen sons and one daughter in addition to a number of other children by his concubines (I Chronicles 3:1–9).

5. Gideon had seventy sons (Judges 8:30).

6. Heman had fourteen sons and three daughters (I Chronicles 25:5).

7. Ibzan had thirty sons and thirty daughters (Judges 12:8, 9).

8. Jair had thirty sons (Judges 10:3, 4).

9. Rehoboam had twenty-eight sons and sixty daughters (II Chronicles 11:21).

10. Shimei had sixteen sons and six daughters (I Chronicles 4:27).

Note: The total number of children that Solomon had with his many wives is not known.

Fasts

The origins of fasting in the Bible are relatively obscure. It appears that, for the most part, fasting in the Bible emerged in response to spiritual needs. Here is a sampling of biblical fasts:

1. **David** fasted as he lamented over Saul's death (II Samuel 1:12) and as he lamented over Abner's death (II Samuel 3:35). David fasted as he lamented over his child's illness (II Samuel 12:16).

2. **Darius** fasted as he worried about Daniel's fate (Daniel 6:18–24).

3. **Elijah** fasted for forty days after fleeing from Jezebel (I Kings 19:17–18).

4. **Esther** fasted as she prayed for her people to be rescued from the malevolent Haman (Esther 4:13–16).

5. **Moses** fasted forty days as he prayed concerning Israel's sin (Deuteronomy 9:9).

6. **Nehemiah** fasted as he wept over the destroyed walls of Jerusalem (Nehemiah 1:4–2:10).

7. **The Ninevites** fasted after they were preached to by Jonah (Jonah 3).

Fires

Numerous instances of fire are found throughout the Bible. Here is a cross section of biblical fires:

1. Fire from heaven destroyed Sodom and Gomorrah (Genesis 19:24).

2. Abraham built a fire upon which to sacrifice Isaac (Genesis 22:7).

3. Moses received God's calling out of the fire of a burning bush that was not consumed (Exodus 3:2).

4. The seventh Egyptian plague included fire (Exodus 9:24).

5. The guiding pillar of fire helped give the Israelites direction in the wilderness at night (Exodus 13:21).

6. Fire appeared at the giving of the Ten Commandments (Exodus 19:8).

7. Fire was ordered by Moses to destroy the golden calf (Exodus 39:20).

8. God sent a fire to consume Aaron's offerings (Leviticus 9:24).

9. A strange fire offered by Nadab and Abihu, sons of Aaron, led to their being punished by God (Leviticus 10:1).

10. The judgment fire of God at Taberah was meant to punish the Israelites (Numbers 11:1).

11. A judgment fire consumed Korah and his 250 followers (Numbers 16:35).

12. A fire was ordered by Joshua to destroy Jericho (Joshua 6:24).

13. A fire was made by Samson to burn the grain fields of the Philistines (Judges 15:5).

14. The fire at Mount Carmel consumed Elijah's offering (I Kings 18:38).

15. A fire destroyed 100 soldiers while protecting Elijah (II Kings 1:7–11).

16. Nebuchadnezzar's fire miraculously did not harm three Hebrew believers (Daniel 3:25).

God's Attributes

The Bible tells us many things about God. The following is a listing of some of them along with references for further study:

1. God is self-existent (Exodus 3:13–14).

2. God is self-sufficient (Psalm 50:10–12).

3. God is eternal (Deuteronomy 33:27).

4. God is infinite (Jeremiah 23:24).

5. God is everywhere (Psalm 139:7–12).

6. God is all-powerful (Genesis 18:14).

7. God is all-knowing (Psalm 139:2–6).

8. God is wise (Proverbs 3:19).

9. God is sovereign (Isaiah 46:9–11).

10. God is incomprehensible (Job 11:7–19).

11. God is holy (Leviticus 19:2).

12. God is righteous and just (Psalm 119:137).

13. God is faithful (Deuteronomy 7:9).

14. God is good (Psalm 107:8).

15. God is merciful (Psalm 103:8–17).

16. God is gracious (Psalm 111:4).

17. God is one (Deuteronomy 6:4–5).

18. God forgives (Exodus 34:7).

God's Names

Various Hebrew terms are used for God throughout the Bible. Some of these are employed in both the generic and the specific sense, while others are used only as the personal name of the God of Israel. Most of these terms were likely also used by the Canaanites to designate their pagan gods. This is not surprising, since on settling in the Promised Land the patriarchs and early Israelites made the language of Canaan their own. The following are some of the names of God that appear in the Bible:

1. *Adonai.* The Hebrew word *adon* means "lord." It is the personal name of the God of Israel, written in the Bible with the four consonants YHWH, referred to as the tetragrammaton (see Genesis 15:2).

2. *Adonai Nissi.* Meaning "God our banner" (Exodus 17:15).

3. *Adonai Rafa.* Meaning "God our Healer" (Exodus 16:26).

4. *Adonai Tzev'ot.* Meaning "Lord of the Celestial Hosts" (Isaiah 6:1–3).

5. *Boray Yisrael.* Creator of Israel (Isaiah 43:15).

6. *Eheyeh asher Eheyeh.* The answer that Moses receives from God when he asks God for the Divine name in the area of the burning bush (Exodus 3:13–14). Often understood as "God will be as God will be," foretelling God's promise of divine power as redeemer and deliverer.

7. *El.* This is the oldest Semitic term for God (Genesis 33:20).

8. *El Berit.* The Divine name *El Berit* (God of the Covenant) occurs only in Judges 9:46, where mention is made of the temple of *El Berit* at Shechem.

9. *El Elyon.* The Hebrew word *elyon* is an adjective meaning "higher" or "upper." When used in reference to God, the word can rightly be translated as "Most High" (Deuteronomy 32:8).

10. *El Olam.* According to Genesis 21:33, "Abraham planted a tamarisk at Beer Sheba and invoked there the name of YHWH, the everlasting God." The Hebrew for "the everlasting God" is *El Olam*, literally, "the God of an indefinitely long time."

11. *El Ro'i.* The divine name *El Ro'i* occurs in Genesis 16:13. After Hagar was driven away by Sarai and fled into the western Negev, at a certain spring or well she had a vision of God, and she called God *El Ro'i*, meaning "God of the Vision" (i.e., who showed Himself to me).

12. *El Shaddai.* According to the literary source of the Torah that the critics call the "priestly document," God "appeared to Abraham, Isaac, and Jacob as 'El Shaddai'" (Exodus 6:3). The traditional English rendering of this term for God is "God Almighty."

13. *Elohim.* The plural of "El," it is also used to denote "gods" and idols.

14. *Kadosh.* Meaning "the Holy One" (Isaiah 40:25).

15. *Melech Yisrael.* Meaning "King of Israel" (Isaiah 44:6).

16. *Ro'ay Yisrael.* Meaning "Shepherd of Israel" (Psalm 80:2).

17. *Tzur.* Meaning "the Rock" (Deuteronomy 32:4).

God's Word

God reveals Himself to people using His words. The following is a listing of references related to the word of God.

1. "Man does not live by bread alone, but by every word that comes from the mouth of God" (Deuteronomy 8:3).

2. "The word is very close to you, in your mouth and in your heart, so that you may do it" (Deuteronomy 30:14).

3. "The word of God is right" (Psalm 33:4).

4. "By the word of God the heavens were fashioned" (Psalm 33:6).

5. "God sent his word and healed them" (Psalm 107:20).

6. "God's word is a lamp unto my feet and a light unto my path" (Psalm 119:105).

7. "God's word runs very swiftly" (Psalm 147:15).

8. "Every word of God is pure" (Proverbs 30:5).

Impersonators

Examples abound in the Bible of the ability of characters to impersonate others. The following are some of the Bible's most well-known impersonators.

1. Sarai posed as Abram's sister in Egypt (Genesis 12:10–20).

2. Rebekah posed as Isaac's sister in Gerar (Genesis 26:6–11).

3. Jacob disguised himself as his brother Esau so well that his father Isaac believed it (Genesis 27:1–29).

4. Leah posed as her sister Rachel when Jacob married her (Genesis 29:21–25).

5. The Gibeonites fooled Joshua by impersonating ambassadors from a distant country (Joshua 9:4–16).

6. David escaped from King Achish by pretending to be a madman (I Samuel 21:12–22:1).

7. Saul disguised himself and put on other raiment as he went out to see the medium at Endor (I Samuel 28:8).

8. Joab convinced the wise woman of Tekoah to pretend to be a mourning widow and to ask for King David's help (II Samuel 14:1–24).

9. Jeroboam's wife disguised herself and went to the prophet Ahijah to find out what the future held, but God told him who she was (I Kings 14:1–6).

10. A prophet disguised himself as a wounded soldier in order to get a point across to King Ahab (I Kings 20:35–43).

11. King Ahab disguised himself when fighting the Syrians, but a fatal arrow killed him anyway (I Kings 22:30–40).

12. King Josiah disguised himself for battle against King Necho of Egypt. He was fatally wounded nonetheless (II Chronicles 35:20–24).

Jerusalem

Jerusalem, the most important city of the Bible, has been the focal point of Jewish religious life and aspirations ever since David made it his city in 1000 B.C.E. Here David and Solomon, Isaiah and Jeremiah, Ezra and Nehemiah lived and labored for their people. So profound is the love of the Jewish people for Jerusalem, and so deep has the Holy City been embedded in Jewish life and lore, that it has been known by seventy endearing names and various other appellations in biblical and postbiblical commentaries. Some of those better known follow with their meanings.

1. *Adonay Yireh* (Genesis 22:14). "The Lord is Seen"

2. *Ariel* (Isaiah 29:1) "Lion of God"

3. *Betulah* (Lamentation 1:16). "Virgin"

4. *Bitzaron* (Zechariah 9:12). "Stronghold"

5. *Drushah* (Isaiah 62:12). "Sought After"

6. *Gai Hizayon* (Isaiah 22:1). "Valley of Vision"

7. *Gilah* (Isaiah 65:18). "Joy"

8. *Ir Elohim* (Psalm 87:2). "City of God"

9. *Ir Haemet* (Zechariah 8:3). "City of Truth"

10. *Jebus* (Judges 19:10). "Lord"

11. *Kir* (Ezekiel 13:14). "City"

12. *Kiriah Alizah* (Isaiah 22:2). "Joyful City"

13. *Kiriah Neemanah* (Isaiah 1:25). "Faithful City"

14. *Kiryat Hanah David* (Isaiah 29:10). "City where David Encamped"

15. *Kiseh Adonai* (Jeremiah 3:17). "Throne of the Lord"

16. *Klilat Yofi* (Lamentations 2:15). "Paragon of Beauty"

17. *Moriah* (Genesis 22:2). "Teacher"

18. *Neveh Tzedek* (Jeremiah 31:22). "Dwelling of Righteousness"

19. *Shalom* (Genesis 14:18). "Peace"

20. *Tzur Hamishor* (Jeremiah 21:13). "Rock of the Plain"

Judges in the Bible

The period of the judges, or civic leaders, begins with the death of Joshua and ends during the lifetime of the prophet Samuel. Here is a list of the judges:

1. Abdon, son of Hillel. Recorded only as having been happy with his children.

2. Barak, son of Abinoam and Deborah. Delivered Israel from vassalage to Jabin, king of Canaan, through the defeat of the army of Jabin's general, Sisera.

3. Ehud, son of Gera. Relieved Israel of vassalage to Eglon, king of Moab.

4. Elon, the Zebulunite. No record exists.

5. Gideon, son of Joash. Smote the Midianites.

6. Ibzan of Bethlehem. Often identified as Boaz, ancestor of David.

7. Jair, the Gileadite. Passed down rule over the cities of Gilead to his sons.

8. Jephthah, the Gileadite. Keeping his rash vow, he sacrificed his own daughter as a victory offering to God.

9. Othniel, son of Kenaz. The first judge to rule during the period of Israelite subjection to Aram.

10. Samson, son of Manoah. Nazirite and warrior, with the strength given him through his long hair he delivered Israel from the Philistines.

11. Samuel, the prophet. The last of the judges and the first of the prophets.

12. Shamgar, son of Anath. Relieved Israel of vassalage to the Philistines.

13. Tola, son of Puah. A very wise judge, according to the sages.

Kings of Israel

After the period of the judges, the kings began to rule in Israel. The profession of king was a combination of judge and military leader. Here is a list of the kings of Israel, beginning with the united monarchy. The death of King Solomon spelled the end of the united Israelite kingdom and its division into Judah in the south and Israel in the north.

UNITED MONARCHY (1020–928 B.C.E.)

1. Saul (1020–1004 B.C.E.) was Israel's first king and helped to unite the tribes of Israel. After a reign of twenty years, he killed himself at the battle of Gilboa.

2. David (1004–965 B.C.E.) was anointed king by Samuel when he was just a child. He is best known for conquering Jerusalem and making it Israel's capital.

3. Solomon (965–928 B.C.E.) was famed for his great wisdom and many wives.

KINGS (AND ONE QUEEN) OF JUDAH
(928–586 B.C.E.)

1. Rehoboam (928–911 B.C.E.) was the son of Solomon and ruled over Judah. He was accused of idolatry, a sin attributed to the influence of his many foreign wives.

2. Aviyam (911–908 B.C.E.) attempted to conquer Israel but advanced only a few miles to Bethel.

3. Asa (908–867 B.C.E.) was a religious reformer who tried to stamp out idolatry.

4. Jehoshaphat (867–846 B.C.E.) strengthened the army and helped to revive commerce.

5. Jehoram (846–843 B.C.E.) was accused of idolatry after he married the daughter of Achab and Jezebel of Israel.

6. Ahaziah (843 B.C.E.) was distinguished by falling through the latticework of an upper room, seriously injuring himself.

7. Athaliah (842–836 B.C.E.) was the only queen either kingdom ever had. She promoted Baal worship.

8. Joash (836–798 B.C.E.) was killed by his own officers.

9. Amaziah (798–769 B.C.E.) was 25 years old when he took a census to conscript an army. In a successful war, he recovered trade routes to the Gulf of Aqaba.

10. Uzziah (769–758 B.C.E.) took the throne at age 16, making Judah more prosperous than it had been since King Solomon.

11. Jothan (758–733 B.C.E.) maintained Judah's prosperity and military advantage.

12. Ahaz (733–727 B.C.E.) was a particularly weak king who indulged in pagan cults.

13. Hezekiah (727–698 B.C.E.) attempted to restore Israelite worship in Jerusalem and received the backing of the prophet Isaiah.

14. Manasseh (698–642 B.C.E.) is noted for the restoration of pagan cults.

15. Amon (641–640 B.C.E.) continued idolatrous practices and was eventually assassinated by his officers.

16. Josiah (639–609 B.C.E.) instituted religious reform.

17. Jehoahaz (609 B.C.E.) tried to be king, but Pharaoh Necho II sent him in chains to Egypt, where he died.

18. Jehoiakim (608–598 B.C.E.) was appointed puppet ruler of Judah by Pharaoh Necho.

19. Jehoiachin (597 B.C.E.) was taken captive to Babylon under the reign of Nebuchadnezzar.

20. Zedekiah (596–586 B.C.E.) rebuilt Jerusalem's defenses and saved the city from the Edomites.

Kings of Israel (928–798 B.C.E.)

1. Jeroboam (928–907 B.C.E.) built a new capital at Tirzeh.

2. Nadav (907–906 B.C.E.) battled with Judah over the location of the border.

3. Baasha (906–883 B.C.E.) unsuccessfully invaded Judah and, in turn, was invaded by Damascus.

4. Elah (883–882 B.C.E.) was murdered by his officer Zimri while drunk.

5. Zimri (882 B.C.E.) ruled for only seven days and died when a burning palace, a fire he had set, collapsed on him.

6. Omri (882–871 B.C.E.) was a great and wise king who made peace with Judah and won back Moab and other lost territories.

7. Ahab (871–852 B.C.E.) was a good ruler who continued Omri's peaceable foreign policy and domestic prosperity.

8. Ahaziah (852–851 B.C.E.), in his first act as king, injured himself by falling from a second story.

9. Jehoram (851–842 B.C.E.) made an abortive attempt to recover Moab.

10. Jehu (842–814 B.C.E.) stamped out Baal worship.

11. Joash (836–798 B.C.E.) was made king when he was 7 years old. Later in his career he repaired the Temple.

12. Jehoahaz (814–800 B.C.E.) punished Jerusalem by breaching the walls and taking treasure and captives.

13. Jeroboam II (784–748 B.C.E.) was a strong ruler who made peace with Judah and recovered territory until

Israel returned to the size it had been during the reign of King David.

14. Zechariah (748–747 B.C.E.) reigned for six months before being assassinated.

15. Shallum (748–747 B.C.E.) reigned one month and was murdered by Menachem.

16. Menachem (747/746–737/736 B.C.E.) went on a killing spree and suppressed all opposition to his reign.

17. Pekachiah (737/736–735/734 B.C.E.) collected tributes for Assyria until he was murdered by one of his army officers.

18. Pekach (735/734–733/732 B.C.E.) attacked Judah and carried off captives.

19. Hoshea (733/732–724/723 B.C.E.) was a puppet king who collected tribute for Assyria.

Last Words

Throughout the Bible many of the characters have an opportunity to utter some final words before their death. Here is a cross section of some of the more well known last statements:

1. **David**. His last words are spoken to Solomon: "I go the way of all the earth: be you strong, and show yourself a man. Keep the charge of the Lord your God, to walk in His ways, to keep His statutes, and His commandments . . ." (I Kings 2:1–9).

2. **Elijah**. While they were waiting for the whirlwind that was to carry Elijah to heaven, Elisha begged him for "a double portion of the spirit." Elijah's last words, just before the chariot of fire appeared, were: "If you see me when I am taken from you, it shall be so unto you. But if not, it shall not be so" (II Kings 2:9–10).

3. **Elisha**. Elisha's last words were angry ones, in which he told Joash to take his arrows and "smite upon the ground." Joash smote three times and waited for Elisha's reaction. Elisha went into a fury and stormed at

the king, saying, "You should have smitten five or six times. Then had you smitten Syria till you had consumed it. Now you shall smite Syria but three times" (II Kings 13:14–19).

4. **Jacob**. "I am to be gathered unto my people. Bury me with my fathers in the cave that is in the field of Ephron the Hittite, . . . which Abraham bought . . . for a possession of a burying place" (Genesis 49:29–30).

5. **Jehoram**. When King Jehoram realized that he was betrayed and about to die at the hands of his own general Jehu, his last thought was for his kinsman Ahaziah, the king of Judah. Jehoram shouted the warning: "There is treachery, O Ahaziah" (II Kings 9:23).

6. **Jezebel**. Jezebel's last words were quite defiant. When Jehu entered the palace gates to kill her, she reminded him of Zimri, a former usurper who had taken the throne by murder and who ended up committing suicide: "Had Zimri peace, who slew his master?" (II Kings 9:31).

7. **Moses**. After Moses blesses the Israelites tribe by tribe, he says the following: "Happy are you O Israel: who is like unto you, O people saved by God, the shield of your help, and who is the sword of your excellency. Your enemies shall be found liars unto you, and you shall tread upon their high places" (Deuteronomy 33:29).

8. **Wife of Pinchas**. Her last words are to name her child Ichabod, saying, "The glory is departed from Israel, for the ark of God is taken" (I Samuel 4:22).

Lepers

In the Bible leprosy was considered one of the most dreaded of all diseases. The rabbis regarded leprosy as a providential affliction in punishment for slander or tale bearing. The Bible (Leviticus 12–15) describes the early symptoms of the disease, its diagnosis, and its treatment. Following is a cross section of those acquiring leprosy in the Bible.

1. Moses put his hand into his bosom. When he took it out his hand was leprous as snow (Exodus 4:6).

2. God spoke to Moses, saying, "Command the children of Israel, that they put out of the camp every leper" (Numbers 5:1–2).

3. Miriam became leprous, white as snow (Numbers 12:10).

4. Naaman, captain of the host of the king of Syria was a leper (II Kings 5:1).

5. Gechazi became a leper after lying to Elisha (II Kings 5:27).

6. There were four leprous men at the entering in of the gate of Samaria (II Kings 7:3).

7. God smote Azariah so that he was a leper unto the day of his death (II Kings 15:5).

8. Uzziah the king was a leper unto the day of his death (II Chronicles 26:21).

Lies

Telling the truth has always been considered an important Jewish value. The Bible warns us to keep far from falsehood. Although telling the truth was a virtue, there were numerous occasions of telling lies in the Bible. The following is a partial listing of them:

1. Abraham's lie to Pharaoh (Genesis 12:13) and to Avimelech (Genesis 20:2).

2. Isaac's lie to Avimelech (Genesis 26:7).

3. Jacob's lie to Isaac (Genesis 27:19).

4. Jacob's sons' lie to Jacob (Genesis 37:32).

5. Laban's lie to Jacob (Genesis 29:18–24).

6. Michal's lie to her father Saul (I Samuel 19:13–17).

7. Potiphar's wife's lie to her husband (Genesis 39:17).

8. Rahav's lie to the Jericho search party (Joshua 2:4).

9. Sarah's lie to God (Genesis 18:15).

10. Saul's lie to David (I Samuel 18:17).

11. The serpent's lie to Eve (Genesis 3:4).

Marriages

Marriage is a sacred duty in the Bible. Throughout the Bible many marriages take place. Here is a cross section of them.

1. Adam to Eve (Genesis 2:21–25)

2. Abraham to Keturah (Genesis 25:1)

3. Ahab to Jezebel (I Kings 16:31)

4. Ahasuerus to Esther (Esther 2:17)

5. Boaz to Ruth (Ruth 4:13)

6. David to Bathsheba (II Samuel 11:27)

7. David to Michal (II Samuel 18:20, 28)

8. Esau to Judith (Genesis 26:34–335)

9. Hosea to Gomer (Hosea 1:2–3)

10. Isaac to Rebekah (Genesis 24:63–67)

11. Jacob to Leah and Rachel (Genesis 29:18–23)

12. Joseph to Asenath (Genesis 41:45)

13. Lamech to Adah and Zilah (Genesis 4:19)

14. Moses to Zipporah (Exodus 2:21)

POLYGAMISTS

The following is a partial list of biblical characters who had more than one wife:

1. Abijah, king of Judah, had fourteen wives (II Chronicles 13:21).

2. Abraham had a wife Sarah and a concubine Hagar (Genesis 16:1–3).

3. David had eight wives (I Samuel 18:27, 25:42–43, II Samuel 3:2–5, 11:27, 12:8).

4. Elkanah, father of Samuel, was the husband of Hannah and Peninah (I Samuel 14:50, II Samuel 3:7).

5. Esau, son of Isaac, had three wives (Genesis 26:34, 28:9).

6. Gideon, Israelite judge, had many wives (Judges 8:30).

7. Jacob had four wives (Genesis 29:15–35, 30:4, 9).

8. Lamech, descendant of Cain, had two wives (Genesis 4:19).

9. Rehoboam, Solomon's son, had eighteen wives and sixty concubines (II Chronicles 11:21).

10. Solomon had 700 wives and 300 concubines (I Kings 11:13).

Miracles

There are numerous miracle stories in the Bible, each of which describes a wondrous event. The following is a cross section of miracles that demonstrate the love of God:

1. Splitting of the Red Sea. The spectacular fleeing of the Israelites from the pursuing Egyptians forms the conclusion of the tale of liberation. God tells Moses, "Lift up your rod and stretch out your hand over the sea and divide it. And the children of Israel shall go into the midst of the sea on dry ground" (Exodus 14:16). Moses follows God's command, a fierce wind parts the sea, and the Israelites are able to cross safely. The entire people of Israel are saved, while the Egyptian army drowns in the sea.

2. Sweetening the waters of Marah. In Exodus 15:23–25, the people of Israel are unable to drink the bitter waters of Marah. The people grumble against Moses, saying, "What shall we drink?" Moses cries out to God, and God shows him a piece of wood. He throws it into the water, and miraculously the water becomes sweet.

3. Heavenly manna. Six weeks after the Israelites have left Egypt, when they are not yet accustomed to life in the wilderness, the provisions they have brought with them are exhausted. It is soon thereafter that there appears on the face of the wilderness a fine, scale-like thing on the ground. Moses explains to them that it is bread that God has given them to eat. It is like coriander seed, white, and has the taste of wafers made with honey (Exodus 16:14–). The manna is miraculously supplied to the Israelites until they enter Canaan and the fruit of the land is available (Joshua 5:12).

4. Water drawn from the rock. Upon realizing, after they have encamped at Rephidim, that there is no water to drink, the Israelites begin to quarrel with Moses, asking him to provide them with water. Hearing their complaints, Moses fears for his life and calls to God, asking for assistance. God then speaks these words to him: "Pass before the people and take with you some of the elders of Israel, and take along the rod with which you struck the Nile, and set out. I will be standing there before you on the rock at Horeb. Strike the rock and water will issue forth from it, and the people will drink." Moses hits the rock and the people are able to drink (Exodus 17:5–6).

In a later story appearing in Numbers 20, Moses is again told that he and Aaron are to take the rod, gather the people, and order the rock to deliver its water. In this story, Moses is ordered to command the rock verbally to spew forth its water. Instead, Moses chooses to strike the rock twice with his rod, and the Israelites are given water. As a result of Moses' striking the rock instead of speaking to it, both he and his brother Aaron are told that they will not lead the Israelites directly into the Promised Land.

5. The serpent of brass heals (Numbers 21:9). In this story, the Israelites speak out against God and Moses, complaining of the miserable food in the wilderness. God sends fiery serpents among the people, who are bitten by them and die. It is then that the Israelites appeal to Moses, having realized their sin by speaking against God. Moses intercedes, and God tells Moses to make a fiery figure and mount it on a standard. If anyone who is bitten looks at the serpent, God says that he or she will recover. Moses makes a copper serpent, and when anyone is bitten by a serpent, that person simply looks at it and miraculously recovers.

6. The parting of the Jordan River (Joshua 3:1–17). In this miracle story, when the Israelites and the priests carrying the Ark of the Covenant come to the Jordan, the priests set their feet into the Jordan and the waters rise up in one heap. All of the people of Israel are able to pass right over on dry ground, as God had promised.

7. The miracle of Daniel's Furnace (Daniel 3:20). In this story, Daniel and his three friends who were exiled to Babylon refuse to bow down before the image that King Nebuchadnezzar had set up. The three are thrown into a blazing furnace, but not even their clothes are singed.

8. Daniel in the Lion's Den. In the sixth chapter of the Book of Daniel, Daniel is accused by his rivals of showing disregard for the Persian King Darius. The King has no choice but to sentence him to death. Daniel is cast into a den of lions, and God sends an angel to close the mouths of the lions. Daniel is miraculously saved.

9. Jonah survives the whale (Book of Jonah.) Ordered by God to prophesy the destruction of Nineveh for its wickedness, Jonah attempts to escape the divine com-

mand by sailing from the Land of Israel. A huge storm severely affects the sailing of the ship, and the sailors appeal to Jonah for guidance. As tensions continue to mount, Jonah is cast into the sea and the sea ceases from raging. It is then that God prepares a large fish that swallows Jonah, who remains in its belly for three days and nights. Jonah prays to God and several days later is miraculously ejected onto dry land.

10. Miracle Pregnancies.

—God closes all the wombs of Avimelech's household because Avimelech had taken Sarah for himself. After Sarah is restored to Abraham, Abraham prays and the women bear children (Genesis 20:17–18).

—Although Sarah is old and unable to bear children, she gives birth to Isaac when she is 90 years old, as God fulfills His promise (Genesis 21:1–5).

—Rebekkah is barren until her husband Isaac prays for her. Then she conceives and gives birth to the twins Jacob and Esau (Genesis 25:21–26).

—God opens the womb of the barren Rachel, and she gives birth to Joseph and Benjamin (Genesis 30:22–24).

—The angel of God appears to Manoah's barren wife, fortelling that she will bear a son (Samson) who would deliver Israel from the Philistines (Judges 13:3, 5).

—God shuts up Hannah's womb, so that she is childless. But then, in answer to Hannah's intense prayer, she gives birth to Samuel (Samuel I:1–20).

—Although her husband is "too old," the Shunammite woman bears a son, thus fulfilling Elisha's word (II Kings 4:13–17).

MIRACLE BIBLE STORIES OF ELIJAH

The Prophet Elijah lived during the reign of King Ahab. Many miracle stories are associated with him, and today he is perhaps the leading miracle man in all of Jewish folklore. Here is a cross section of Elijah's biblical miracle stories.

1. Elijah and the widow (I Kings 17). In this miracle story there is a wondrous feeding of a widow.

2. Ahaziah's troops are consumed by fire (II Kings 1:10).

3. Elijah obtains rain in the time of King Ahab (I Kings 18:41).

4. The descent of fire upon the altar of Mount Carmel (I Kings 18:38).

5. The splitting of the waters of the Jordan (II Kings 2:8, 14).

6. The cake baked on hot stones and the cruse of water that sustains Elijah for forty days (I Kings 19:1–8).

7. The feeding of Elijah by ravens (I Kings 17:6).

8. Vision of God at Mount Horeb (I Kings 19:10–12).

9. Elijah's ascent to heaven in a whirlwind (II Kings 2:9–11).

MIRACLE STORIES OF ELISHA

1. The healing of the waters of Jericho (II Kings 2:19–22).

2. The killing of the youths by the bears (II Kings 2:23–24).

3. The filling of the trenches with water, without wind or rain (II Kings 3:20).

4. God's blessing of increase from the pot of oil of Obadiah's widow (II Kings 4:1–7).

5. The birth of the son of the Shunammite woman and his resuscitation (II Kings 4:8–34).

6. The curing of the bitter pottage of the sons of the prophets (II Kings 4:38–41).

7. The healing of Naaman's leprosy (II Kings 5:1–14).

8. The floating of an axhead upon the water (II Kings 6:1–7).

9. The smiting of the Samarian army with blindness and the restoration of sight through the intercession of prayer (II Kings 6:18–20).

10. The confusion caused by God in the Aramean camp (II Kings 7:6).

11. The resurrection of the man who came in contact with Elisha's bones (II Kings 13:21).

Murderers

The sixth of the Ten Commandments states, "You shall not kill." Nothing could be further from the truth in biblical times. The following is a list of those who did kill others in the Bible:

1. A servant killed Joash because of his evil ways (II Kings 12:20–21).

2. Absalom killed Amnon to avenge the rape of Tamar (II Samuel 13:28–29).

3. Cain killed Abel out of envy (Genesis 4:8).

4. David had Uriah killed to conceal his adultery with Bat Sheba (II Samuel 12:9).

5. Ehud killed Eglon of Moab (Judges 3:21).

6. Hoshea killed Pekah to take his throne (II Kings 15:30).

7. Ishmael killed Gedaliah as an act of anarchy (II Kings 25:25).

155

8. Israel killed the High Priest Zechariah (II Chronicles 24:20–21).

9. Jael killed Sisera (Judges 4:17–21).

10. Jehu killed Ahaziah because he was with Jehoram (II Kings 9:27).

11. Jehu killed Jehoram to fulfill a prophecy and rid the country of Ahab's dynasty (II Kings 9:24).

12. Jezebel had Nabot killed to obtain his land for Ahab (II Kings 21:13).

13. Joab killed Abner to eliminate competition (II Samuel 3:27).

14. Joab killed Absalom for revenge (II Samuel 18:14).

15. Joab killed Amasa (II Samuel 20:10).

16. Lamech killed a young man out of pride (Genesis 4:23).

17. Moses killed an Egyptian (Exodus 2:12).

18. Nebuchadnezzar killed Zedekiah's son to punish him for his rebellion (Jeremiah 39:6).

19. Pekah killed Pekahiah to take his throne (II Kings 15:25).

20. Rechab and Baanah killed Ish Boshet to get in David's good graces (II Samuel 4:6).

21. Shallum killed Zechariah in order to take away his throne (II Kings 15:10).

22. Simeon and Levi killed Hamor and Shechem for revenge of the rape of their sister Dinah (Genesis 34:26).

23. Zimri killed Elah to steal his throne (I Kings 16:10).

Musicians and Musical Instruments

The biblical record is full of the idea that it is natural for people to burst spontaneously into song when especially moved by the wonders of God's creation or when God delivers a person from harm. The following is a cross section of biblical musicians:

Musicians

    1. **Asaph**. Asaph played the cymbals (I Chronicles 16:5).

    2. **Benaiah** and **Yahaziel**. Benaiah and Yahaziel played the trumpet (I Chronicles 16:6).

    3. **David**. Known for his harp playing, he played the instrument for Saul, causing the evil spirit to depart from him (I Samuel 16:23).

    4. **Heman**. Heman played and led the players of the trumpet and cymbals (I Chronicles 16:42).

5. **Israelite women**. They came out of the cities, singing and dancing to meet King Saul, with tabrets, joy, and musical instruments (I Samuel 18:6).

6. **Jeduthun**. Jeduthun was one of King David's chief musicians (I Chronicles 16:42).

7. **Jeiel**. Jeiel played the psaltery and harp (I Chronicles 16:5).

8. **King Solomon**. He wrote 1,005 songs (I Kings 4:32).

9. **Miriam**. When she crossed the Red Sea, she and all the women went out with timbrels and dances (Exodus 15:20–21).

10. **Yuval**. He was the father of all those who play the harp and organ (Genesis 4:21).

Musical Instruments

Some nineteen identifiable terms for musical instruments appear in the Bible. Some scholars hold that other terms, notably those appearing in the headings of the Psalms, also refer to instruments. However, it is more probable, according to Bible scholars, that they provide instructions regarding a particular melody. Here is a brief description of some of the Bible's instruments:

1. *Chalil*. (I Samuel 10:5) is a double-pipe wind instrument, probably having one melody and one drone pipe.

2. *Chatzotzerah*. This is identified with the trumpet and was made of precious metal, generally silver. It is

mentioned some thirty times in the Bible, where its introduction in Israelite ceremonies is attributed to Moses. The silver trumpet Moses was commanded to make (Numbers 10:2) served ritual, military, and administrative-organizational functions.

3. *Kinnor*. This is a stringed instrument in the lyre family. It was played by King David and thus was held in particular honor by the Levites (Psalm 150).

4. *Mena'anayim*. Mentioned only in II Samuel 6:5, they are listed among the instruments played during King David's transport of the Ark to Jerusalem. They are a type of percussion instrument.

5. *Metziltayim*. Mentioned in Ezra 3:10, these are a type of cymbals.

6. *Minnim*. Mentioned in Psalm 150, this was a stringed instrument, possibly a lute.

7. *Nevel*. Mentioned in II Samuel 6:5 and I Kings 10:12, this is a type of lyre.

8. *Pa'amon*. Usually defined as a bell, it is mentioned only in connection with the service of the Tabernacle (Exodus 28:33–34).

9. *Shalishim*. Mentioned only in I Samuel 18:6–7, they were thought to be a type of cymbal played by women.

10. *Shofar*. The is the horn of the ram and is the only biblical instrument to have survived in Jewish usage. In the Bible it functioned as a signaling instrument, especially in wartime. It also made a famous appearance at the battle of Jericho (Joshua 6:6–20).

11. *Tof*. One of the most ancient of instruments, it is a type of drum that was frequently played by women and associated with the dance (Exodus 15:20–21, Judges 11:34).

12. *Ugav*. Perhaps it was a harp, although its real nature is uncertain (Psalm 150).

13. Other instruments. Daniel 3:5 describes in Aramaic an orchestra of the Babylonian king. It includes the *karna, mashrokita, kaitros, sabbecha, pesanterin*, and *symponyah*.

Numbers

Ever since primitive people learned to count on their fingers, numbers have had a special significance. Among various peoples and religions, they have even assumed sacred proportions, some being considered lucky and others being unlucky. The Jewish Bible is replete with numbers that are sometimes to be taken at face value but likely to be more noteworthy for their symbolic nuances. Biblical numbers range from 1 (Genesis 1:5) to 100,000,000 (Daniel 7:10) The following are some popular biblical numbers and their references in the Bible.

THE NUMBER TWO

1. The animals came to Noah into the ark, **two** of each of all flesh (Genesis 7:15).
2. When God finished speaking with Moses on Mount Sinai, He gave Moses the **two** tablets of the Pact (Exodus 31:18).

3. If, however, a leper is poor and his means are insufficient, he shall take . . . **two** turteldoves or **two** pigeons, depending on his means (Leviticus 14:21–22).

4. "Joshua, the son of Nun, secretly sent **two** spies from Shittim" (Joshua 2:1).

5. "There will I meet you, and I will speak with you from above the ark cover, from between the **two** cherubim which are upon the ark of the covenant" (Exodus 25:22).

THE NUMBER THREE

1. When Abraham asked God how he would know that he possessed the land, God answered as follows: "Bring me a **three**-year old heifer, a **three**-year old she-goat, a **three**-year old ram, a turtledove, and a young bird" (Genesis 15:9).

2. For **three** years the eating of the fruit of a newly planted tree was forbidden (Leviticus 19:23).

3. "**Three** times a year shall you hold a festival for me. You shall observe the Feast of Unleavened Bread . . . the Feast of the Harvest . . . and the Feast of the Ingathering" (Exodus 23:14–16).

4. **Three** times a day Daniel kneeled upon his knees and prayed (Daniel 6:11).

5. Elijah stretched over the child **three** times, and cried to God saying, "O God, let this child's life return to his body!" (I Kings 17:21)

6. The woman conceived and bore a son [Moses], and when she saw how beautiful he was, she hid him for **three** months (Exodus 2:2).

THE NUMBER FOUR

1. A river issues from Eden to water the garden, and then it divides and becomes **four** branches (Genesis 2:10).

2. "How much less should any escape now that I have let loose against Jerusalem all **four** of my terrible punishments—the sword, famine, wild beasts, and pestilence" (Ezekiel 14:21).

3. "I looked up, and I saw **four** horns" (Zechariah 2:1).

4. "Cast four rings for it, to be attached to its **four** feet" (Exodus 25:12).

5. I shall bring **four** winds against Elam from the **four** quarters of heaven, and scatter them to all those winds (Jeremiah 49:36).

THE NUMBER FIVE

1. "Let **five** of the remaining horses that are still here be taken" (II Kings 7:13).

2. "Benjamin's portion was **five** times that of anyone else" (Genesis 43:34).

3. "He disposed the lever stands, **five** at the right side of the house and **five** at its left side" (I Kings 7:39).

4. "When a man steals an ox or a sheep, and slaughters it or sells it, he shall pay **five** oxen for the ox" (Exodus 21:37).

5. "And the redemption price of the 273 Israelite firstborn over and above the number of Levites, take **five** shekels per head" (Numbers 3:47).

6. **"Five** of you shall give chase to one hundred" (Leviticus 26:8).

THE NUMBER SIX

1. **Six** days shall you labor and do all manner of work (Exodus 20:9).

2. When you acquire a Hebrew slave, he shall serve for **six** years (Exodus 21:2).

3. **Six** steps led up to the throne (I Kings 10:19).

4. Seraphim stood in attendance with Him. Each of them had **six** wings (Isaiah 6:2).

5. Ruth was given **six** measures of barley (Ruth 3:15).

THE NUMBER SEVEN

1. Of every clean animal you shall take **seven** pairs (Genesis 7:2).

2. Abraham then set **seven** ewes of the flock by themselves (Genesis 21:28).

3. **"Seven** days you shall make offerings by fire to God" (Leviticus 23:8).

4. Bilaam said to Balak, "Build me **seven** altars and have **seven** bulls and **seven** rams ready here for me" (Numbers 23:1).

5. The lamps on it are **seven** in number, and the lamps above it have **seven** pipes (Zechariah 4:2).

6. "The priest shall dip his finger in the blood and

sprinkle of the blood **seven** times before God" (Leviticus 4:6).

7. Jacob served **seven** years for Rachel (Genesis 29:20).

8. "Let Pharaoh take steps to appoint overseers over the land and organize the land of Egypt in the **seven** years of plenty" (Genesis 41:34).

THE NUMBER TEN

1. "Then the servant took **ten** of his master's camels and set out" (Genesis 24:10).

2. **Ten** princes with him, one prince for every division of all the tribes of Israel (Joshua 22:14).

3. Micah said to him, "Remain with me and become for me a father and a priest, and I will give you **ten** shekels of silver for the year" (Judges 17:10–11).

4. **Ten** men were found among them that said to Ishmael, "Slay us not" (Jeremiah 41:8).

5. And he said, "Let not the Lord be angry, and I will speak yet but this once: Peradventure there will be found there **ten**." And God said: "I will not destroy for the sake of **ten**." (Genesis 18:32).

THE NUMBER FORTY

1. The span of human life is three times **forty** years (Genesis 6:3).

2. Caleb said, "I was **forty** years old when Moses the

servant of God sent me from Kadesh Barnea to spy out the land" (Joshua 14:7).

3. "And the Israelites ate manna for **forty** years, until they came to a settled land" (Exodus 16:35).

4. "For in seven days' time I will make it rain upon the earth, **forty** days and **forty** nights, and I will blot out from the earth all existence that I created" (Genesis 7:4).

5. "At the end of **forty** days, they [the spies] returned from scouting the land" (Numbers 13:25).

6. "The Philistine stepped forward morning and evening and took his stand for **forty** days" (I Samuel 17:16).

7. Jonah started out and made his way into the city the distance of one day's walk, and proclaimed, "**Forty** days more, and Nineveh shall be overthrown" (Jonah 3:4).

8. "He may be given up to **forty** lashes" (Deuteronomy 25:3).

9. "Next he measured the depth of the hall, **forty** cubits" (Ezekiel 41:2).

Plagues

The Bible is filled with horrific accounts of damaging plagues, all causing havoc upon nations as well as individuals. Following is a cross section of them.

PLAGUES UPON NATIONS

1. Egypt

   —Blood (Exodus 7:20)
   —Frogs (Exodus 8:6)
   —Lice (Exodus 8:17)
   —Flies (Exodus 8:24)
   —Cattle disease (Exodus 9:3)
   —Boils (Exodus 9:10)
   —Hail (Exodus 9:24)
   —Locusts (Exodus 10:13)
   —Darkness (Exodus 10:22)
   —Death of Firstborn (Exodus 12:29)

169

2. Israel

   —Death by sword, due to idolatry (Exodus 32:27).
   —Death by fire, due to complaining (Numbers 11:11).
   —Death by an unnamed plague, due to lust (Numbers 11:31–35).
   —Death by earthquake for rebellion (Numbers 16:32).
   —Death by poisonous serpents for rebellion (Numbers 21:6).
   —Death for immorality (Numbers 25:9).
   —Death for looking into the Ark of God (I Samuel 6:19).

3. Philistia—A plague of tumors, for capturing the Ark of God (I Samuel 5:8–9).

4. Syria—A plague of blindness for attacking Israel (II Kings 6:18).

PLAGUES UPON INDIVIDUALS

1. Upon Pharaoh for attempting to marry Sarah (Genesis 12:17).

2. Upon Avimelech for attempting to marry Sarah (Genesis 20:18).

3. Upon Moses to show him God's power. (Exodus 4:6–7).

4. Upon Nadav and Avihu for offering strange fire (Leviticus 10:1–2).

5. Upon Miriam for criticizing Moses (Numbers 12:1–10).

6. Upon Saul for his disobedience (I Samuel 16:14).

7. Upon Nabal for his hatred of David (I Samuel 25:38).

8. Upon Jeroboam for his false religion (I Kings 13:4).

9. Upon Gechazi for lying (II Kings 5:20–27).

10. Upon Uzziah for attempting to assume priestly duties (II Chronicles 26:16–21).

Plants

The Bible mentions about 100 names of plants, the bulk of them in the land of Israel, the others being trees of Lebanon and tropical plants that yielded an aromatic substance or were used in incense. Although the biblical plants are chiefly those of economic importance, they are to a large extent mentioned fortuitously. Here is a sampling of the plants mentioned in the Bible:

Name	Hebrew Name	Reference
Acacia	*Sheeta*	Exodus 26:15
Almond	*Shaked*	Jeremiah 1:1
Aloe	*Ahaleem*	Proverbs 7:17
Apple	*Tapuach*	Joel 1:12
Balsam	*Bosem*	Song of Songs 5:1
Barley	*S'orah*	Exodus 9:31
Bean	*Pole*	II Samuel 17:28
Boxthorn	*Atad*	Genesis 50:10–11
Broom plant	*Rotem*	I Kings 19:4–5
Castor oil plant	*Keekayon*	Jonah 4:6
Cedar	*Erez*	Isaiah 2:13
Cinnamon	*Keenamon*	Exodus 30:23

Name	Hebrew Name	Reference
Citron	*Eytz Hadar*	Leviticus 23:40
Coriander	*Gad*	Exodus 16:31
Cotton	*Karpas*	Esther 1:6
Cucumber	*Paku'ote*	II Kings 4:39
Cumin	*Kamon*	Isaiah 2:25
Cypress	*Gofer*	Genesis 6:14
Ebony	*Havneem*	Ezekiel 27:15
Fennel flower	*Ketzach*	Isaiah 28:25
Fig	*Sheekma*	I Kings 10:27
Flax	*Peeshtan*	Joshua 2:6
Frankincense	*Levonah*	Exodus 30:34
Garlic	*Shoom*	Numbers 11:5
Grape vine	*Gefen*	Genesis 40:9
Hemlock	*Rosh*	Deuteronomy 29:17
Henna	*Kofer*	Song of Songs 1:14
Juniper	*Brosh*	Isaiah 14:8
Laurel	*Oren*	Isaiah 44:14
Leek	*Chatzeer*	Numbers 11:5
Lentil	*Adasheem*	Genesis 25:34
Lily	*Shoshan*	Hosea 14:6
Mandrake	*Dooda'eem*	Genesis 30:14–16
Melon	*Keeshoot*	Numbers 11:5
Myrrh	*Mor*	Exodus 30:23
Myrtle	*Hadas*	Isaiah 41:19
Narcissus	*Shoshanat*	Song of Songs 2:1
Nettle	*Seerpad*	Isaiah 55:13
Oak	*Alon*	Genesis 35:8
Olive	*Zayeet*	Deuteronomy 6:11
Onion	*Batzal*	Numbers 11:5
Palm	*Tamar*	Exodus 15:27
Papyrus	*Gomeh*	Exodus 2:3
Pine	*Teehar*	Isaiah 41:19
Pistachio	*Botna*	Genesis 43:11
Pomegranate	*Reemon*	Numbers 20:5
Poplar	*Tzaftzafa*	Ezekiel 17:5
Raspberry	*Sneh*	Exodus 3:2–4

Name	Hebrew Name	Reference
Reed	*Kaney*	Isaiah 19:6
Saltbush	*Maluach*	Job 30:4
Tamarisk	*Ayshel*	Genesis 21:33
Terebinth	*Ayla*	Genesis 35:4
Thistle	*Dardar*	Genesis 3:18
Thorn	*Charool*	Zephaniah 2:9
Walnut	*Egoz*	Song of Songs 6:11
Watermelon	*Avateeach*	Numbers 11:5
Wheat	*Cheeta*	Exodus 9:32
Willow	*Aravah*	Leviticus 23:40
Wormwood	*La'anah*	Deuteronomy 29:17

Prayers

Although sacrifices were the primary mode of communication with God in the Bible, prayer also begins to appear as another form of communication between God and human beings. For the most part, biblical prayer consists of personal, spontaneous pleas to God, since fixed liturgy did not exist during these times. What follows is a cross section of some of the earliest recorded prayers in the Bible. Each prayer will be listed in the following sequence:

Prayer. The words of the prayer and its biblical source
Object. The goal or object of the prayer
Speaker. The person who uttered the prayer
Outcome. The outcome or result of the prayer

1. Prayer: "And Abraham drew near and said: 'Will You sweep away the righteous with the wicked? Peradventure there are fifty righteous within the city, will You indeed sweep away and not forgive the place for the fifty righteous that are therein?'" (Genesis 18:23–24).

177

—Object. To petition God to forgive the sin of the Sodomites for the sake of righteous people.

—Speaker. Abraham

—Outcome. God agrees that He will forgive if ten righteous souls are found.

2. Prayer: "And he said: 'O God, the God of my master Abraham, send me, I pray You, good speed this day, and show kindness to my master Abraham'" (Genesis 24:12).

—Object. To petition God to help in the search for a suitable wife for Abraham's son, Isaac.

—Speaker. Eliezer, Abraham's trustworthy servant.

—Outcome. Eliezer finds Rebekah, whom Isaac marries.

3. Prayer. Isaac entreats God for his wife, because she is barren (Genesis 25:21).

—Object. Isaac petitions God that his barren wife, Rebekah, be able to bare children.

—Speaker. Isaac

—Outcome. Rebekah gives birth to twin sons, Jacob and Esau.

4. Prayer. "And Jacob vowed a vow, saying: "If God be with me, and will keep me in this way that I go, and will give me bread to eat and raiment to put on so that I come back to my father's house in peace, then shall the Lord be my god'" (Genesis 28:20–21).

—Object. This conditional vow asks God for prosperity in return for devotion to God.

—Speaker. Jacob

—Outcome. No immediate outcome, but Jacob ultimately becomes Israel and the third patriarch of the Israelites.

5. Prayer. "And Jacob said: 'O God of my father Abraham, And God of my father Isaac, O God, who said to me: Return to your country, to your kindred, and I will do you good. I am not worthy of all the mercies that You have shown your servant. For with my staff I passed over this Jordan, and now I am become two camps. Deliver me, I pray You, from the hand of Esau . . .'" (Genesis 32:10–11).

—Object. Petitioning of God to be protected from Esau.

—Speaker. Jacob, Esau's brother.

—Outcome. Jacob and Esau reconcile and Esau forgives Jacob.

6. Prayer. "And he said: 'O God, send I pray You, by the hand of him whom You will send'" (Exodus 4:13).

—Object: Discouraged by his mission, Moses petitions God to choose an alternate leader.

—Speaker. Moses

—Outcome. God becomes angry because of the obstinate reluctance of Moses to accept his charge.

7. Prayer. "Who is like you, O God, among the mighty? Who is like You, glorious in holiness, revered in praise, doing wonders?" (Exodus 15:11).

—Object. Moses and the children of Israel sing this praise of God after successfully being liberated from Egypt and crossing the Red Sea.

—Speaker. Moses and the Israelites

—Outcome. As a result of the miracle of the splitting of the Red Sea, the Israelites are saved and sing a song to God.

8. Prayer. "And Moses cried to God saying: 'What shall I do to this people? They are almost ready to stone me" (Exodus 17:4).

—Object. The Israelites grow angry in the desert because of their lack of water and blame Moses for their predicament.

—Speaker. Moses

—Outcome. God hears the plea of Moses and tells him to strike a rock with his rod. Moses does so and water comes forth so that the people are able to quench their thirst.

9. Prayer. "Moses returned to the people and said, 'This people have sinned a great sin, and have made for themselves a god out of gold. Yet now, if You will forgive their sin. If not, blot me, I pray You, out of Your book which you have written'" (Exodus 32:31–32).

—Object. Moses entreats God to forgive the Israelites for their sins of constructing a golden calf.

—Speaker. Moses

—Outcome. God will not permit Moses to suffer vicariously for the sins of his people, God then punishes the Israelites.

10. Prayer. "I pray to You, if I have found grace in Your sight, show me now Your ways, so that I may know You, to the end that I may find grace in Your sight . . ." (Exodus 33:13).

Object. Moses entreats God and asks that God reveal His attributes to him.
—Speaker. Moses
—Outcome. God reveals thirteen Divine attributes.

11. Prayer. "The Lord bless you and keep you. The Lord make His face to shine on you and be gracious to you. The Lord lift up His countenance and give you peace" (Numbers 6:24–26).

—Object. A formula for a blessing of the Israelite people.
—Speaker. God speaks to Moses.
—Outcome. This blessing becomes the official priestly blessing with which the priests bless the people of Israel. It continues to be used in modern times as the family blessing when parents bless their children on Friday evening.

12. Prayer. "Moses cried to God saying: 'Heal her now God, I beseech You'" (Numbers 12:13).

—Object. Moses cries to God to heal his sister Miriam, who has been struck with the dreaded disease of leprosy.
—Speaker. Moses
—Outcome. Miriam is cured after seven days.

13. Prayer. "And now, I pray You, let the power of God be great, according as You have spoken saying, 'God is slow to anger and abounding in lovingkindness. . . . Pardon, I pray You, the sin of this people according to the greatness of Your lovingkindness, and according as You have forgiven this people, from Egypt even until now'" (Numbers 14:17–19).

—Object. Moses petitions God to forgive the Israelites for believing the spies who presented the negative report.

—Speaker. Moses

—Outcome. God pardons the people of Israel.

14. Prayer. "And I besought God at that time saying: 'O God, You have begun to show your servant Your greatness, and Your strong hand. For what God is there in heaven or on earth, that can do according to Your works, and according to Your mighty acts? Let me go over, I pray You, and see the good land that is beyond the Jordan'" (Deuteronomy 3:23–25).

—Object. Moses prays to God that he may see and step foot into the Promised Land.

—Speaker. Moses

—Outcome. God tells Moses to no longer petition Him about this matter. Moses ultimately sees the Promised Land from the banks of the Jordan River, but is not permitted to enter it.

15. Prayer. "The Rock, His work is perfect, for all God's ways are justice. A God of faithfulness and without sin. Just and right is God" (Deuteronomy 32:4).

—Object. Moses ends his life of service to God and Israel with a hymn of joy in which he praises God for His dependability and justice.

—Speaker. Moses

—Outcome. Moses is told that he will be allowed to see the Promised Land from a distance.

16. Prayer. "And she made this vow: 'O God of Hosts, if You will look upon the suffering of Your maidservant and will remember me and not forget Your maidservant, and if You will grant Your maidservant a male child, I will dedicate him to God for all the days of his life'" (I Samuel 1:11).

—Object. The barren Hannah petitions God that she may be able to give birth to a son, who she vows will be dedicated and totally devoted to God's service.

—Speaker. Hannah

—Outcome. Hannah gives birth to Samuel.

17. Prayer. "Then Solomon stood before the altar of God in the presence of the whole community of Israel. He spread the palms of his hands toward heaven and said, 'O Lord, God of Israel, in the heavens above and on the earth below there is no God like You, who keep Your gracious covenant with Your servants and when they walk before You in wholehearted devotion'" (I Kings 8:22–23).

—Object. The entreatment of God, asking that God's presence be brought to earth, focused in the Jerusalem Temple

—Speaker. Solomon

—Outcome. God causes His Presence to dwell in the Temple.

18. Prayer. "When it was time to present the meal offering, the prophet Elijah came forward and said, 'O Lord, God of Abraham, Isaac, and Israel. Let it be known today that You are God in Israel and that I am Your servant, and that I have done all these things at Your request. Answer me O God, that this people may know that You, O God, are God'" (I Kings 19:36–37).

—Object. Entreating God to destroy the pagan god Baal.
—Speaker. The prophet Elijah
—Outcome. Fire from God descends and consumes Elijah's burnt offering, thus proving to the people that there is only one single God in the world.

19. Prayer. "Jonah prayed to God from the belly of the fish. He said 'In my trouble I called to God and He answered me'" (Jonah 2:2–3).

—Object. Jonah, having been swallowed by the big fish, prays to God for deliverance.
—Speaker. Jonah
—Outcome. God hears Jonah's prayer and commands the fish to spew Jonah forth onto dry land.

20. Prayer. "I prayed to Adonai my God, making confession thus: 'O God, great and awesome One, who remains faithful to His covenant with those who love Him and keep His commandment. We have sinned, we have gone astray. . . . The shame O God is on us . . .

because we have sinned against You. To the Lord our God belong mercy and forgiveness, for we have rebelled against You'" (Daniel 9:4–9).

—Object. That God will rebuild Jerusalem.
—Speaker. Daniel
—Outcome. Jerusalem is rebuilt in seventy weeks.

Priesthood

When the children of Israel were charged to be a "kingdom of priests and a holy nation," it was the duty of the *Kohanim* ("priests"), the descendants of Aaron and his priestly sons, to offer up all sacrifices and carry out various ritual tasks, first in the Tabernacle and then in the Temple in Jerusalem. The priests were also obligated to instruct the people in God's commandments and to concern themselves with the people's health, physical welfare, and moral well-being. The office of the High Priest entailed the observance of special rules concerning ritual purity and defilement, cleanliness, pedigree, and prohibited marriages.

The following is a list of the High Priests from Aaron until the destruction of the First Temple in Jerusalem:

1. **Aaron**. The elder brother of Moses, Aaron was the first High Priest. The Tabernacle was erected during his lifetime (Numbers 7:8).

2. **Eleazar**. The third son of Aaron, Eleazar was anointed High Priest after the deaths of his brothers Nadav and Avihu. He served as High Priest under Moses

and Joshua and participated in the conquest of Canaan (Numbers 20:25–29).

3. **Pinchas**. Pinchas turned away God's wrath from the children of Israel by his display of religious zeal in killing Zimri, son of Salu, and Cozbi, daughter of Zur, a Midianite woman (Numbers 25:7–9).

4. **Abishua**. Abishua was the first High Priest to be anointed in the land of Canaan (I Chronicles 5:30–31, 6:35).

5. **Bukki**. The great-grandson of Aaron, Bukki was the second High Priest to be anointed in Canaan (Ezra 7:3, I Chronicles 5:31).

6. **Uzzi**. According to tradition, Uzzi was the last of the High Priests of the line of Pinchas to serve in the Tabernacle. The office was transferred to the family of Ithamar and was not restored to the family of Pinchas until the reign of King Solomon, when Zadok was anointed High Priest. Uzzi is mentioned in the Books of Ezra (7:4) and I Chronicles (5:31–32).

7. **Eli**. The first member of the family of Ithamar to serve as High Priest, Eli officiated in the Tabernacle at Shiloh. In addition to being a High Priest, Eli also served as a judge (I Samuel 4:18).

8. **Achituv**. Son of Pinchas, grandson of Eli, brother of Ichabod, and father of Ahimelech, he ministered during the reign of King Saul (I Samuel 14:3, 22:9, 11–12, 20).

9. **Achiyah**. The son of Achituv, Achiyah apparently was High Priest during the reign of Saul. He is mentioned as having taken part in the wars of Michmas, in which he wore the *ephod* in the camp of Saul (I Samuel 14:3).

10. **Achimelech**. According to tradition, Achimelech was the son of Achituv and the brother of Achiyah. He was the High Priest in the temple of Nov during the reign

of King Saul (I Samuel 21–22), and he supervised eighty-five priests who wore linen *ephods* and were all members of the family of Eli (I Samuel 22:15–18).

11. **Aviatar**. The sole survivor of Saul's slaughter of the priests of Nov, Aviatar, son of Avimelech, fled to David and served as the latter's priest throughout all of his wanderings (I Kings 2:26). With Aviatar, the line of High Priests of the family of Ithamar came to an end.

12. **Zadok**. According to tradition, with Zadok the office of High Priest reverted to the family of Pinchas. Zadok is mentioned in the Bible as a priest together with Aviatar (II Samuel 8:17).

13. **Achimaatz**. He became High Priest after the death of his father Zadok and was said to have ministered during the reign of Rechoboam, son of Solomon (II Samuel 18:20).

14. **Azariah**. He was the son of Achimaatz (I Chronicles 5:35) and was said to have served as High Priest during the reign of Avihu, son of Rechoboam.

15. **Yochanan**. Yochanan was the son of Azariah (I Chronicles 5:35) and served as High Priest during the reign of King Yehoshaphat.

16. **Azariah II**. Of this High Priest the Bible says, "he it is that executed the priest's office in the house of Solomon built in Jerusalem" (I Chronicles 5:36).

17. **Amariah**. The son of Azariah (I Chronicles 5:37), he was High Priest during the reign of Yehoshaphat. He was appointed to supervise the judges in Jerusalem in all that pertained to religious matters.

18. **Yehoiada**. He ministered as High Priest during the reign of Athaliah. He saved Yoash, an infant of the royal line, from Athaliah, who murdered all the other members of the royal family (II Kings 11–12).

19. **Azariah III**. He was High Priest during the reign of King Uzziah (II Chronicles 26:18–19).

20. **Uriyahu**. He was High Priest during the reign of King Ahaz (II Kings 16:10–11).

21. **Shallum**. The father of Hilkiah the High Priest, Shallum was also known as Meshullam. With him, the High Priesthood reverted to the line of the house of Zadok.

22. **Hilkiah**. When the Temple was repaired in the eighteenth year of the reign of King Josiah, Hilkiah the High Priest found there the Book of Law. King Josiah read the contents to the people and then commanded Hilkiah to remove from the Temple all the vessels that were made for the idols (II Kings 22:2–20).

23. **Azariah IV**. Azariah, son of Hilkiah the High Priest, ministered during the reign of King Yehoiakim (I Chronicles 6:13).

24. **Seraiah**. After the destruction of Jerusalem and the Temple by Nebuchadnezzar, King of Babylon, in the days of King Zedekiah, Nebuzaradan, the captain of the host, exiled and "took Seraiah the chief priest, and Zephaniah, the second priest . . . and brought them to the King of Babylon. The King of Babylon smote them" (II Kings 25:18–21).

25. **Yehotzadak**. The son of Seraiah, he was the last of the High Priests during the First Temple period. He was killed by the Babylonian king (I Chronicles 5:41).

QUALIFICATIONS OF THE HIGH PRIEST

In order to qualify for the High Priesthood, the following criteria had to be met:

1. The High Priest had to be the eldest son of the line of Aaron and could have no blemish (Leviticus 21:16–23).

2. The High Priest was forbidden to marry a widow, a divorcee, a profaned woman, or a harlot. He had to wed only a virgin of his own people (Leviticus 21:14).

3. The High Priest was not to exhibit any signs of mourning. He was not to allow his hair to grow too much, tear his clothes, leave the sanctuary during the service, or defile himself for any dead body, including the bodies of his father and mother (Leviticus 21:10–12).

4. When entering the tent of meeting, the High Priest had to wash his hands and feet with water (Exodus 30:19–21).

MINISTERIAL DUTIES OF THE HIGH PRIEST

1. First, Aaron offered incense on the golden altar each morning when he prepared the lamps, and also each evening when he lit the lamps (Exodus 30:7–8).

2. It was his duty to carry out the prescribed ritual on the Day of Atonement (Leviticus 16).

3. He arranged the shewbread on the Sabbath and ate it in a holy place (Leviticus 24:9).

4. Whenever he was unclean he had to separate himself from the holy things of the children of Israel (Leviticus 22:1–3).

5. If the High Priest sinned unintentionally, he was to sacrifice a bullock as a sin offering (Leviticus 4:3–13).

6. It was the duty of the High Priest to eat the remains of the meal offerings of the children of Israel in a holy place (Leviticus 6:9).

7. The High Priest was to be present when a king was crowned or a leader chosen (Numbers 27:19–21).

8. The High Priest was to oversee the distribution of war booty (Leviticus 31:21–28).

9. When the camp journeyed forward, Aaron and his sons had to dismantle and carry the Tabernacle and its implements (Numbers 4:5–16).

10. The High Priests had to bless the people (Numbers 6:23–27).

11. The High Priests were in charge of the holy things and the altar (Numbers 18:5).

GENERAL DUTIES OF THE PRIESTS

In addition to the aforementioned duties of the High Priest, the common priests had the following obligations:

1. To be among the descendants of Aaron and physically unblemished (Leviticus 21:16–23).

2. Not to defile themselves for any corpse, except when the dead person was a mother, father, son, daughter, brother, wife, or virgin sister (Leviticus 21:1–5).

3. Not to marry a profaned woman, a divorced woman, or a harlot (Leviticus 21:7).

4. To keep charge of holy things and guard the altar (Numbers 18:5).

5. To kindle the fire on the altar and keep the fire burning (Leviticus 6:2).

6. To collect half of the blood of certain sacrifices in basins and sprinkle the remaining blood on the altar (Exodus 24:6).

7. To set the wood in order upon the fire of the altar and make the various sections of the offering smoke (Leviticus 1:5–10).

8. To pinch off the head of any bird offered as a sacrifice, and drain its blood on the side of the altar (Leviticus 5:9).

9. To make the daily offering of one lamb in the morning and one in the evening (Numbers 28:3).

10. To offer up the meal offering and smoke a portion of it on the altar as a memorial (Leviticus 2:1–2).

11. To sprinkle the blood of the peace offering about the altar (Leviticus 3:1–3).

12. To sacrifice the sin offering of one who has committed an unintentional sin (Leviticus 4:30).

13. To eat of the guilt offering in a holy place (Leviticus 7:6).

14. To offer up the meal offering (Leviticus 6:7–8).

15. To eat the shewbread in a holy place (Leviticus 24:9).

16. To make atonement for the woman who had given birth and who had already fulfilled the days of her purification (Leviticus 12:6–7).

17. To ascertain when the leprous spots had departed from the leper (Leviticus 14:3–4), to purify the leper (Leviticus 14:6–7), to determine whether a house was afflicted with leprosy (Leviticus 14:33–47), to make atonement for the house, and to purify it (Leviticus 14:49–53).

18. To make atonement for any man suffering from a

flow and to purify him (Leviticus 15:14–15) and to purify any woman who was unclean (Leviticus 15:29–30).

19. To offer the sheaf of first fruits (Leviticus 23:10–11).

20. To estimate the sum to be paid by a person who made a vow and could not afford the regular valuation (Leviticus 27:8).

21. To prepare the water of bitterness used in testing a woman accused of adultery and to conduct the prescribed ritual (Numbers 5:12–31).

22. To make atonement for the Nazirite when the latter's period of abstinence had come to an end (Numbers 6:9–13).

23. To offer up the sin offering and burnt offering of the Nazirite when the period of the latter's consecration had been fulfilled (Numbers 6:14–15).

24. To sound the silver trumpets on the required occasions (Numbers 10:8).

25. To atone for the entire congregation or for an individual in the case of sins committed through error (Numbers 15:24–27).

26. To prepare the prescription of the spices (I Chronicles 9:30).

27. To prepare the waters of sprinkling (Numbers 19:1–11).

28. To serve as judges when people sought them out to settle disagreements (Deuteronomy 17:9).

29. To encourage the soldiers who were going out to battle and to address the people and their officers (Deuteronomy 20:2–3).

30. To supervise the breaking of the neck of a heifer

after a corpse was found in a field and the identity of the murderer could not be ascertained (Deuteronomy 21:1–9).

31. To flay the burnt offering (II Chronicles 29:34) and slaughter the Paschal lamb (Ezra 6:20).

Promises

The Bible is filled with references to conditional promises. The following are thirty biblical promises accompanied by their conditions and references.

Promise	Condition	Reference
1. "Blessed shall be the fruit of your body"	"You will hearken to God's voice"	Deut. 28:2, 4
2. Your children shall be delivered	You are righteous	Prov. 11:21
3. A nation is exalted	By righteousness	Prov. 14:34
4. "He shall be like a tree planted by rivers of water that brings forth fruit"	The person whose delight is in the law	Psalm 1:1–3
5. God shall strengthen you heart	"Wait upon the Lord"	Psalm 27:14
6. "I shall not want"	"The Lord is my Shepherd"	Psalm 23:1

197

Promise	Condition	Reference
7. All of God's paths are mercy and truth	Keep God's covenant and God's testimonies	Psalm 25:10
8. None shall be desolate	Trust in God	Psalm 34:22
9. God will preserve him and keep him alive	One who considers the poor	Psalm 41:1–2
10. He glorifies God	Who so offers praise	Psalm 51:17
11. "No evil shall befall you"	"Because you have made God your habitation"	Psalm 91:10
12. You are blessed	God chastens you	Psalm 94:12
13. One shall not be afraid of evil tidings	One's heart is fixed and trusts God	Psalm 112:7
14. "They will have great peace"	Those who love Your law	Psalm 119:165
15. God gives them sleep	His beloved	Psalm 127:2
16. They shall prosper	Those praying for the peace of Jerusalem	Psalm 122:6
17. "God is near unto all"	"Who call upon Him in truth"	Psalm 145:18
18. "They shall reap in joy"	"Those that sow in tears"	Psalm 126:5
19. "The moon shall not smite you by night"	"God is your keeper"	Psalm 121:5
20. "You will prolong your days on earth"	"Keep God's statutes"	Deut. 4:40

Promise	Condition	Reference
21. God will remove sickness from you	Keep the commandments	Deut. 7:15
22. God will give you rain in its season	Keep God's commandments	Deut. 28:9
23. God will honor them	Those that honor God	I Sam. 2:30
24. God will be found by you	If you seek God	II Chronicles 15:2
25. You shall find wisdom	Love wisdom and seek it	Prov. 8:17
26. The just shall be delivered	Through knowledge	Prov. 11:9
27. Happy is the person	One having mercy on the poor	Prov. 14:21
28. "He shall obtain favor of God"	"A good person"	Prov. 12:22
29. He is wise	One that wins souls	Prov. 11:30
30. "God will repay you"	"Those having pity on the poor"	Prov. 19:17

Prophets

The Hebrew word for prophet, *navi*, signifies a spokesperson, one who speaks for a divine power to human beings. Foreseeing the outcome of national crises and evil practices, the prophets fearlessly criticized the morals of their own day while teaching a nobler way of living. Their message was usually one of warning and exhortation, including a prediction of coming events in the near or distant future.

The following is a listing of the forty-eight male prophets and seven female prophets according to Rashi (*Megillah* 14, *Halachot Gedolot* and *Seder Olam*)

MALE PROPHETS

1. **Abraham**. The son of Terach and a descendant of Eber, Abraham was the father of the Israelite nation and the first to preach monotheism to the world. He was the first of the three patriarchs, the first Hebrew to settle in Canaan, and the first person to whom the land of Israel was promised for eternity.

2. **Aaron**. Aaron, brother of Moses, served as an intermediary between Moses and Pharaoh because of his

eloquence. After the Tabernacle was built, the priesthood was promised to Aaron and his descendants for eternity (Exodus, Leviticus and Numbers).

3. **Ahijah the Shilonite**. Ahijah was active toward the end of Solomon's reign. Speaking in God's name, he prophesied the division of the kingdom "because they have forsaken Me . . . and they have not walked in My ways, to do that which is right in My eyes, and to keep My statutes and My ordinances, as did David" (I Kings 11:33). He also urged Jeroboam to accept the kingship over the ten tribes.

4. **Amos**. A native of Tekoa in Judah, this minor prophet prophesied in the days of Uzziah, Jeroboam II, Jotham, Ahaz, and Hezekiah. He was a herdsman by trade, and the first prophet whose utterances have been transmitted to us in a separate book.

5. **Amoz**. According to the sages, he was the brother of King Amaziah. He opposed the importing of troops from the Northern Kingdom to aid Judah (II Chronicles 25:15–16).

6. **Azariah, son of Oded**. During the reign of Asa, king of Judah, Azariah prophesied, "God is with you, while you are with Him. And if you seek Him, He will be found, but if not He will forsake you. . . . Be strong, and let not your hands be slack, for your work shall be rewarded" (II Chronicles 15:1–2, 7). The prophet's words had an effect on Asa, who removed the detestable idols from the land of Judah and Benjamin and from the cities that he had conquered in the hill country of Ephraim.

7. **Baruch, son of Neriah**. The scribe and student of Jeremiah, Baruch "wrote from the mouth of Jeremiah all the words of the Lord, which God had spoken to him, upon a roll of a book" (Jeremiah 36:4).

8. **Chaggai**. This post-exilic prophet, whose book is the tenth of the books of the minor prophets, called for the rebuilding of the Temple.

9. **Chanani the Seer**. He rebuked Asa, king of Judah, for relying on the King of Aram when in danger, and not upon God (II Chronicles 16).

10. **David**. The rabbinic sages observed that David, too, was a prophet because the Bible says, "whom David and Samuel the seer did ordain in their office" (I Chronicles 9:22). It is in reference to them, as well as to Nathan and Gad, that the sages said, "The first prophets established the twenty-four watches of priestly duty" (*Talmud Taanit* 26).

11. **Eli the Priest**. He was the predecessor of Samuel, the last of the judges, and was the last High Priest in the Tabernacle of Shiloh. Eli was revered by all, and his blessing was prized as one that came from the lips of a holy man of God (I Samuel 1:17).

12. **Eliezer, son of Dodavahu**. A Judean prophet, Eliezer told Jehoshaphat, "Because you have joined yourself with Ahaziah, God has made a breach in your works." Jehoshaphat, refusing to heed the prophet's words, made an agreement with the king of Israel to have ships built in Ezion-geber. However, before the vessels were able to sail for Tarshish, their destination, they were destroyed (II Chronicles 20:35–37).

13. **Elijah**. Elijah, a native of Gilead, prophesied and brought miracles in the kingdom of Ephraim during the reigns of Ahab and his son Ahaziah. He waged a ceaseless struggle against Jezebel and the Baal cult which she had brought to Israel from her birthplace (I Kings 19:1–21).

14. **Elisha**. The son of Shaphat, Elisha was the dis-

ciple and successor of Elijah. He had an extraordinary career, performing even more miracles than did Elijah. For example, he spread out the mantle of his master and crossed the Jordan dry-shod (II Kings 2:8). He purified the fountain in Jericho (II Kings 2:19–22) and miraculously increased a widow's supply of oil (II Kings 4:1–7).

15. **Elkanah**. He was the son of Jeruhum, a family of the tribe of Levi (I Chronicles 6:19–24). According to rabbinic tradition (*Talmud Megillah* 14), he was one of the major prophets, unparalleled in his generation.

16. **Ezekiel**. The third of the three major prophets, Ezekiel witnessed the destruction of Jerusalem and Judea and went into exile to Babylonia. His prophecies have great poetic beauty and mystical power. The most famous chapter in the book that bears his name, Chapter 37, describes his symbolic vision of a valley of dry bones that are resurrected, symbolizing the rebirth of Israel.

17. **Gad the Seer**. The Bible refers to Gad as both prophet and seer (I Chronicles 29:29). He accompanied and advised David during the latter's wanderings (I Samuel 22:5) and also helped David organize the Levitical singers in the Temple (I Chronicles 23:27).

18. **Habakkuk**. His book is the eighth of the books of the minor prophets. It is an outcry against the victory of the Chaldeans and the rule of iniquity in the world. It concludes with God's reply and a description of the Day of the Lord.

19. **Hoshea**. He was the first man to symbolize, through his personal life, Israel's relationship to God. His book is one of the minor prophetic books.

20. **Iddo the Seer**. According to the sages, Iddo preached during the reign of Jeroboam, son of Nebat. It was he who came from Judah to Bethel and prophesied

the destruction of the altar that Jeroboam had built there and had sacrificed upon: "O altar . . . ; Behold, a son shall be born to the house of David, Josiah by name; and upon you shall he sacrifice the priests of the high places" (I Kings 13:2).

21. **Isaac**. The only son of Abraham by his wife Sarah, Isaac was the second of the patriarchs. Bound and readied for sacrifice at God's command, he was released at the calling of God's angel.

22. **Isaiah**. He prophesied from the year of Uzziah's death until the beginning of Manasseh's reign. Considered one of the three major classical prophets, he was the first prophet to declare that idolatry and evil would one day cease to exist. (Book of Isaiah)

23. **Jacob**. The son of Isaac, Jacob was the third of the patriarchs and father of the twelve tribes of Israel. He struggled to preserve the spiritual heritage of Abraham, although he was constantly plagued by the contention of his sons and neighbors.

24. **Jehu son of Chanani**. Prophesying during the reign of Asa, Jehu declared that Baasa, ruler of the Northern Kingdom, would suffer Jeroboam's fate. Jehu also wrote the chronicles of Jehoshaphat (II Chronicles 20:34).

25. **Jeremiah**. This major prophet with his own book belonged to a priestly family of Anatot near Jerusalem. He witnessed the tragic events in the history of Judea that ended in the destruction of Jerusalem. His prophecies foretold the doom of his people as punishment for their sins.

26. **Joel**. Second in the order of the twelve minor prophets, Joel called the people of Judea to repent because the Day of Judgment was at hand (Book of Joel).

27. **Jonah, son of Amittai**. According to the book that

bears his name, Jonah was sent to Nineveh to make the people repent of their evildoing. Jonah fled the country, only to be swallowed by a large fish. In the end he was forced to come to Nineveh and successfully aroused its inhabitants to repentance.

28. **Joshua**. The son of Nun, Joshua belonged to the tribe of Ephraim. He led the Israelites in battle in the desert and defeated Amalek in Rephidim (Exodus 17:8).

29. **Machseiah**. He was the father of Neriah and grandfather of Baruch, the scribe of Jeremiah (Jeremiah 32:12).

30. **Malachi**. The last of the biblical prophets, he protests in his book against transgressions in matters of sacrifice and tithes and complains of mixed and broken marriages.

31. **Micah**. He was a minor prophet who spoke out against the social evils of his time, maintaining that they would bring about the nation's downfall. Perhaps his most famous statement was the following: "It has been told, O man, what is good, and what God requires of you: do justly, love mercy, and walk humbly with your God" (Micah 6:8).

32. **Micaiah, son of Imlah**. In the days of Ahab, Micaiah was the only true prophet among some 400 court prophets who told the King whatever he wished to hear (I Kings 22:8). He is one of the first prophets actually to behold God and the heavenly host: "I saw God sitting on His throne, and all the heavenly host standing by Him on His right hand and on His left" (I Kings 22:19).

33. **Mordecai**. A descendant of Kish, he lived in Shushan and reared Esther, his cousin. Because he frequented the courtyard of the royal palace, he overheard a plot to kill the king and by reporting it saved the latter's

life. With Esther's help, Mordecai was able to help to thwart the evil Haman's schemes and bring retribution upon the enemies of Israel (Book of Esther).

34. **Moses**. Moses is considered the greatest of the prophets. Of him the Bible says, "And there has not arisen a prophet since in Israel like Moses, whom God knew face to face" (Deuteronomy 34:10). Moses had a strong influence on all the prophets who followed him and is Israel's lawgiver for all time.

35. **Nahum**. Nahum lived during the reign of Manasseh. One of the minor prophets after whom a book is named, he foretold the fall of Nineveh.

36. **Nathan the Prophet**. Nathan was a prophet in the generation that followed Samuel. He admonished David fearlessly for the latter's misconduct with Bathsheba (II Samuel 12). He was also one of the organizers of the Temple service (I Chronicles 29:29).

37. **Neriah**. Neriah, according to the rabbinic sages, was the father of Baruch and one of the eight prophets descended from Rahab (Jeremiah 36:4).

38. **Obadiah**. Obadiah was the fourth of the so-called twelve minor prophets. His one-chapter book contains only twenty-one verses. In it he predicts the destruction of Edom and severely condemns the Edomites for having refused to assist Jerusalem in the days of calamity, and he expresses the conviction that they will be treated measure for measure, since they helped the Babylonians to bring about the downfall of Judea.

39. **Oded**. Oded prophesied in Samaria during the reign of Ahaz, King of Judah, and Pekah, son of Remaliah, King of Israel. When the Israelites returned from Judah with many prisoners, Oded went out and urged them in God's name to restore their captives to their

native land. His words had a telling effect, and the leaders of Ephraim did not bring any captives back to Samaria (II Chronicles 28:9–15).

40. **Pinchas**. He was the grandson of Aaron. In reward for his zealous action against Zimri, he and his descendants were promised the priesthood (Numbers 25).

41. **Samuel**. He was the son of Elkanah and the last judge of Israel. As a child he served in the Temple at Shiloh, where he had been brought by his mother. When he reached manhood he attained fame as a prophet throughout the land.

42. **Seraiah, son of Neriah**. According to the sages, Seraiah prophesied during the second year of Darius' reign. He appears in the fifty-first chapter of the Book of Jeremiah.

43. **Shemaiah**. A Judean, Shemaiah prophesied during the reign of Rehoboam when the latter mustered his army in hopes of regaining his sovereignty over the Northern Kingdom. Shemaiah, speaking in God's name, warned him not to wage war: "You shall not go up, nor fight against your brothers the children of Israel, . . . for this thing is of Me." Rehoboam heeded the prophet's words and sent his forces home (I Kings 12:22–24).

44. **Solomon**. The rabbinic sages included Solomon among the prophets because of his dream at Gibeon wherein God appeared to him and said, "Ask what I shall give you." And Solomon requested "an understanding heart" to judge the people (I Kings 3:5, 9).

45. **Uriah, son of Shemaiah**. A native of Kiriath-jearim, Uriah prophesied during the reign of Jehoiakim. He foretold the destruction of the city and the country in much the same manner as did Jeremiah (Book of Jeremiah).

46. **Yechaziel the Levite**. "Then upon Yechaziel the son of Zechariah, the son of Benaiah, the son of Jeiel, the son of Mattaniah, the Levite, of the sons of Asaph, came the spirit of God" (II Chronicles 20:14). Yechaziel encouraged Jehoshaphat prior to the battle against Ammon, Moab, and Seir, saying, "Fear not, nor be dismayed. Tomorrow go out against them, for God is with you" (II Chronicles 20:17).

47. **Zechariah**. This minor prophet's prophecies are concerned with contemporary events and foretell the ingathering of the exiles and the expansion of Jerusalem (Book of Zechariah).

48. **Zephaniah**. The prophecies of this minor prophet were mostly eschatological. Described in his book is the Day of the Lord, when God will punish all the wicked and will be universally acknowledged.

FEMALE PROPHETS

The roster of prophets of Israel reveals that the Jewish woman occupied a place of prominence even in the period of earliest biblical antiquity. Distinguished indeed was her contribution in the shaping of the national and ethical character of the male Jew through her constant strengthening of his will to triumphant achievement in times of crisis. According to the *Talmud Sotah* 11b, "because of the merit of the righteous women who lived in that generation were the Israelites redeemed from Egypt."

According to the medieval biblical commentator Rashi, in addition to the forty-eight male prophets previously enumerated, there were also seven female prophets in Israel.

1. Abigail. The Bible records that Abigail prophesied to David: "The Lord will certainly make my lord a sure house. . . . And it shall come to pass, when the Lord shall have done to my lord according to all the good that He hath spoken concerning you, and shall have appointed you prince over Israel, do not let this be a cause of stumbling" (I Samuel 25:28–31).

2. Channah. She was the mother of the prophet Samuel.

3. Chuldah. The wife of Shallu, she lived near the courts of learning in Jerusalem during the reign of Josiah (II Kings 22:14). The sages (*Talmud Megillah* 14b) declared that Chuldah was one of the three prophets of that generation, the other two being Zephaniah and Jeremiah.

4. Deborah. The Bible refers to Deborah as "a prophet, the wife of Lapidot." She fought a famous battle against Sisera and successfully defeated his army.

5. Esther. The rabbis regarded Esther as a prophet because the Bible says of her: "Esther put on her royal apparel" (Esther 5:1). This was interpreted to mean that she was clothed with the divine spirit, as it is written: "Then the spirit clothed Amasai" (I Chronicle 12:19; cf. *Talmud Megillah* 14b)

6. Miriam. The Bible explicitly refers to Miriam as a prophet: "And Miriam the prophet . . . took the timbrel." She was the sister of Moses, the greatest prophet to have ever lived.

7. Sarah. Sarah, the wife of Abraham, bore Isaac. Today she is also considered one of the four Jewish biblical matriarchs.

Proverbs

The fifteenth book of the Bible is the Book of Proverbs. Many of the sayings in this book concern industry, sobriety, honesty, caution, and learning. Its purpose is "to make man know wisdom and instruction, comprehend words of understanding, and take the instruction of acting wisely with justice and righteousness" (Proverbs 1:2–4). Following are selections from the Book of Proverbs.

ON WISDOM

1. "The fear of God is the beginning of knowledge" (Prov. 1:7).
2. "Whosoever loves knowledge loves correction; but one that is brutish hates reproof" (Prov. 12:1).
3. "In a multitude of counselors there is victory" (Prov. 24:6).

SOCIETY AND FAMILY

1. "He that spares his rod hates his son" (Prov. 13:24).

2. "A good name is rather to be chosen than great riches" (Prov. 22:1).

3. "My son, hear the instruction of your father, and forsake not the teaching of your mother" (Prov. 1:8).

4. "A righteous person regards the life of his beast" (Prov. 12:10).

5. "Better is a dinner of herbs where love is present, than a stalled ox and hatred therewith" (Prov. 15:17).

6. "There are friends that one has to his own hurt. But there is a friend that sticks closer than a brother" (Prov. 18:24).

7. "Train up a child in the way he should go, and even when he is old, he will not depart from it" (Prov. 22:6).

8. "When the righteous are increased, the people rejoice; but when the wicked dominate, the people sigh" (Prov. 29:2).

9. "There are four things which are little upon the earth, but they are exceedingly wise: the ants are a people not strong, yet they provide their food in the summer; the rock badgers are but a feeble folk, yet they make their houses in the crags; the locusts have no king, yet they go forth by bands; the spider you cannot take with the hands, yet he is in kings' palaces" (Prov. 30:24–28).

10. "There is not a just person upon earth that does good and does not sin" (Prov. 7:20).

11. "The race is not to the swift, nor the battle to the strong" (Prov. 9:11).

WISE ADVICE

1. "For in much wisdom is much vexation, and one that increases knowledge increases sorrow" (Prov. 1:18).

2. "Be not rash with your mouth, and let not your heart be hasty to utter a word before God; for God is in heaven, and you upon earth; therefore let your words be few" (Prov. 5:1).

3. "It is better to hear the rebuke of the wise than for a person to hear the song of fools" (Prov. 7:5).

4. "Be not overly righteous. Neither make yourself overwise. For why should you destroy yourself?" (Prov. 7:16).

5. "Wisdom is better than strength; nevertheless the poor person's wisdom is despised and his words are not heard" (Prov. 10:1).

6. "Cast your bread upon the water, for you shall find it after many days" (Prov. 11:1).

MORAL INTEGRITY

1. "Go to the ant, you sluggard, consider her ways and be wise" (Prov. 6:6).

2. "A soft answer turns away wrath" (Prov. 15:1).

3. "Death and life are in the power of the tongue" (Prov. 18:21).

4. "The wicked flees when no person pursues" (Prov. 28:1).

5. "Hate stirs up strife, but love covers all transgressions" (Prov. 10:2).

6. "Better is a little with righteousness than great revenues with injustice" (Prov. 16:8).

7. "One that is slow to anger is better than the mighty" (Prov. 16:32).

8. "Do not rejoice when your enemy falls, and let not your heart be glad when he stumbles" (Prov. 24:17).

9. "A word fitly spoken is like apples of gold in settings of silver" (Prov. 25:1).

Queens in the Bible

The following is a partial listing of biblical queens:

1. **Abigail** became wife of David after her husband Nabal died (I Samuel 25:39).

2. **Athalia** attempted to destroy all of the royal seed of the house of Judah (II Chronicles 22:10).

3. **Batsheba** became David's wife after he had her husband Uriah murdered (II Samuel 11:15).

4. **Belshazzar's queen** (unnamed) brought Daniel's prophetic gift to her husband's attention (Daniel 5:10).

5. Ahasuerus loved **Esther** above all other women and made her queen instead of Vashti (Esther 2:17).

6. **Jezebel** married King Ahab and caused him to worship Baal (I Kings 16:31).

7. **Michal**, daughter of Saul, eventually scorned her husband King David (I Samuel 18:20, II Samuel 6:16).

8. When the **Queen of Sheba** heard of the fame of Solomon, she came to test him with difficult questions (I Kings 10:1).

9. **Tachpenes** was the wife of Pharaoh (I Kings 11:19).

10. Queen **Vashti** refused to come at Ahasuerus' command to show the people her beauty (Esther 11:11–12).

Record Setters

Here is a list of biblical characters who possessed unique characteristics:

1. **Cruelest.** King Manasseh, who shed blood from one end of Judah to the other (II Chronicles 33:1–13).

2. **Earliest.** Adam, the world's first human being (Genesis 2:7).

3. **Fastest.** Asahel, described as "light of foot as a wild roe" (II Samuel 2:18).

4. **Fattest.** Eglon, the Moabite king. He was killed by Ehud the judge (Judges 3:17).

5. **Oldest human**. Methuselah, son of Enoch, who died at age 969 (Genesis 5:27).

6. **Strongest human**. Samson, the Nazirite, whom God used to deliver the Israelites from the hands of the Philistines (Judges 14:6).

7. **Richest.** King Solomon (I Kings 10:23).

8. **Tallest.** Goliath, more than nine feet in height. He was killed by David (I Samuel 17:4).

9. **Most beautiful.** Queen Esther, who saved her people from the wicked Haman (Book of Esther).

10. **Most humble.** Moses, the greatest biblical prophet (Numbers 12:3).

11. **Most in love.** Jacob, who agreed to work seven years to attain the hand of Rachel (Gen. 29:30).

12. **Most persecuted.** Job, who lost all of his possessions (Book of Job).

13. **Most rash.** Jephthah, who vowed to offer a special sacrifice if God would allow him to win in a battle. He sacrificed his own daughter (Judges 11:1–33).

Sacrifices

The Hebrew word *korban* ("sacrifice"), literally meaning "to bring near" or "to approach," occurs some eighty times in the Bible, especially in the Books of Leviticus and Numbers. A sacrifice was thus a means by which to approach God, to obtain God's favor, and to atone for the sins of the sacrificer. The first sacrifices recorded in the Bible were offered by Cain ("fruit of the soil" and Abel ("the choicest of the firstborn of the flock") in Genesis 4:4. Noah made an offering of which the Bible stresses its pleasant odor (Genesis 8:20).

Sacrifices can be divided into various categories: propitiatory and dedicatory offerings, burnt offerings, meal offerings, libation offerings, fellowship offerings, peace offerings, thanksgiving offerings, wave offerings, votive offerings, freewill offerings, and ordination offerings. The following is a summary of these offerings:

1. **Burnt Offerings**. An *olah* (meaning "to go up") used these animals: bulls, sheep or goats, and birds (Leviticus 1:3–17). A continual burnt offering (*olah*

tamid in Hebrew) was made twice daily in biblical times. It consisted of a male lamb that was sacrificed both morning and evening (Exodus 29:38–42). Various purification rituals called for burnt offerings: after childbirth (Leviticus 12:6–8), unclean issues (Leviticus 15:14–15), and hemorrhages (Leviticus 15:28–30).

2. **Dedicatory Offerings**. This category of sacrificial offering reflects the more universal idea of offerings in general. It represented the act of committal that should follow the repentance expressed by the sin and guilt offerings, thus opening the way to the communal sacrifices that could follow. (I Kings 8:62–64)

3. **Fellowship Offerings**. This category of sacrificial offering consisted of those offerings that expressed a voluntary desire on the part of the offered. With few exceptions they were not required by explicit rules, but were permitted on the condition that the sacrificer had met with the requirements of penitence. This offering was often accompanied by a burnt offering (Numbers 6:17).

4. **Freewill Offering**. Called a *nedavah*, this was the minimum offering that one could bring to the holy convocations that took place on the three Pilgrim Festivals. Like the votive offering, it could be a burnt offering as well as a peace offering (Leviticus 22:17–24).

5. **Libation Offerings**. A libation (*nesech* in Hebrew) normally accompanied the burnt and the peace offerings (Numbers 15:1–10). The libation, a drink offering of wine, was considered an additional "pleasing odor" offering (Numbers 15:7), and different amounts of wine were used to accompany different animals. Libation offerings in the Bible are mentioned in connection with the Sabbath (Numbers 28:9), the New Moon (Numbers

28:14), Shavuot (Numbers 29:18), and Passover (Numbers 28:16–29).

6. **Meal Offerings**. A regular accompaniment to the animal sacrifices was the meal offering (*mincha* in Hebrew). The meal offering usually consisted of a mixture of fine flour, oil, and frankincense. It took the appearance of baked loaves or wafers. The meal offering usually accompanied the burnt offering rendered after joyous occasions such as the cleansing of a leper (Leviticus 14:10) and the successful consummation of a Nazirite vow (Numbers 6:15).

7. **Ordination Offering**. This type of offering, called *milluim*, meaning "to fill the hand," was used for the consecration of a person to God's service (Exodus 28:41). The details of the ritual are spelled out in Exodus 29:19–34 as Moses appears in the role of the officiant of the ordination of his brother Aaron and his sons.

8. **Peace Offerings**. Called *shelamim* in Hebrew, the peace offerings were the basic sacrifice of all communal sacrifices. Any domesticated animal was allowed to be used as a peace offering, which always concluded with some type of communal meal. The peace offering was specified only for the celebration of Shavuot (Leviticus 23:19–20), in the ritual for the completion of a Nazirite vow (Numbers 6:17–20), and at the installation of the priests (Exodus 29:19–34). National events that called for the peace offering included the successful completion of a military campaign (I Samuel 11:15), the end of a famine (II Samuel 24:25), and the praising of a candidate for the kingship (I Kings 1:9).

9. **Propitiatory Offerings**. In this category are the sin offering (*chattat* in Hebrew) and the guilt offering, (*asham* in Hebrew). The sin offering was suited to the

rank and circumstance of the person who offered it. The High Priest brought a young bull (Leviticus 4:3) while a commoner brought a female goat (Leviticus 4:28).

10. **Thanksgiving Offering**. Known in Hebrew as a *zevach*, this was the most frequently mentioned type of peace offering (Leviticus 7:12–13).

11. **Votive Offering**. Called a *neder* in Hebrew, meaning "a vow," this was usually a peace offering and sometimes a burnt offering. An example of the votive offering was the vow of a Nazirite that was consummated by a peace offering (Numbers 6:17–20).

12. **Wave Offering**. Known in Hebrew as a *tenufah*, the priest's portion of the peace offering was "waved" before God in an act that demonstrated that the offering belonged to God. The waving was only a preliminary to sacrificing the animal or grain offering on the altar fire (Exodus 29:24).

Sexual Terms

In Judaism the sex impulse is not thought to be evil but is considered a holy urge in that it fulfills the commandment of God to bring children into the world. Licit sexual practice is a sacred duty and a sanctified one. Marriage is conceived as the safeguard of the sex act, and violations are subject to punishment. Following is a list of biblical sexual terms.

Term	Hebrew	Translation	Reference
Genitals	*Basar*	Nakedness	Lev. 15:2
Sexual Intercourse	*Ervah*	Flesh	Lev. 18:6
Male Organ	*Shofacha*	Pour out	Deut. 23:1
Sex Act	*Ervah*	Approach	Lev. 18:4
	Shachav	Lie with	Lev. 18:22
	Yadah	To know	Gen. 4:1
Semen	*Zerah*	Seed	Lev. 22:4
Womb	*Rachem*	Womb	Numbers 12:12
Breast	*Shad*	Breast	Song of Songs 1:13
Sexual Organ	*Yarek*	Loin	Gen. 46:26

Staffs, Sticks, and Rods

Staffs, sticks, and rods often play important roles in various biblical narratives. Sometimes they even seem to take on supernatural qualities. The following are twelve famous staffs, sticks, or rods:

1. Jacob used rods in an attempt to control the breeding of animals (Genesis 30:27).

2. Jacob carried a staff with him over the Jordan (Genesis 32:10).

3. Moses turned his staff into a serpent (Exodus 4:2).

4. Aaron's rod was used to swallow up the rods-turned-snakes of the Egyptian magicians (Exodus 7:12).

5. Moses used his staff to help bring the ten plagues upon Egypt (Exodus 7:19).

6. Moses used his staff to strike the rock (Exodus 17:6–7).

7. Aaron's rod was used to demonstrate God's blessing upon him as the rod blossomed (Numbers 17:8).

8. Balaam used a staff to beat his donkey (Numbers 22:27).

9. A staff was used by an angel to consume Gideon's offering (Judges 6:21).

10. A rod was used by Jonathan to secure honey from the hive (I Samuel 14:27).

11. A stick used by Elisha caused an ax head to float (II Kings 6:6).

12. Two sticks were used by the prophet Ezekiel to predict the eventual union of Israel's twelve tribes (Ezekiel 37:16–28).

Taxation

Biblical records do not contain a detailed account of fiscal policy among the Israelites. However, the scattered references to direct and indirect taxes in the Bible are sufficient evidence of the existence of an organized revenue system during the time of the monarchy. Here are some examples of biblical taxation methods:

1. Half-shekel tax. While still in the desert on their way to Canaan, the Israelites were required to pay a half shekel per person. This was used to finance the construction of the sanctuary, while at the same time, the number of half shekels collected constituted a form of census of the people (Exodus 30:11–16).
2. Taxes imposed by a king on the people. In the period of the judges there was enumerated a long catalogue of taxes that a king would impose upon the people, including a tithe on grain, wine, and flocks; a levy on fields, vineyards, and olive orchards; and forced labor (I Samuel 8:9–17).
3. David's census in order to list property for taxation

purposes. The prerequisite for a workable taxation policy is a census of the population. King David ordered "a numbering of the people" (II Samuel 24:1–9), and while Joab, in his final report to the king, gave only the total number of all the able men "who drew the sword," it may be assumed that the object of the census was to list the property of the individual householders for taxation purposes.

4. Solomon's taxation system. Solomon perfected the system of taxation by dividing the country into twelve administrative districts and appointing a "prefect" over each one (I Kings 4:7–19).

5. Menachem's levy. Menachem's levy of fifty shekels per capita on 60,000 wealthy citizens in Israel is mentioned in II Kings 15:19–20.

6. Jehoiakim's assessment. His assessment was based upon the personal fortunes of the people (II Kings 23:35).

7. Tax on wheat. The Book of Amos (5:11) has a reference to taxes on wheat.

8. Tolls on imported goods. Israelite kings levied a toll on imported goods and on products in transit (I Kings 10:14–15).

9. Taxes of the Persian government. According to a reference in Ezra 4:13, the Persian government imposed upon the people three kinds of levies called *mindah, belo,* and *halach.* These are Babylonian technical terms for a variety of taxes.

Ten Commandments

The most famous of the 613 commandments are the Ten Commandments that Moses received on Mount Sinai (Exodus 20). In Temple times, they were read as an official part of the prayer service. Today, they are customarily read in the Bible portion of *Yitro* and on the spring harvest festival of Shavuot.

1. I am the Lord your God who brought you out of the land of Egypt, out of the house of bondage.

2. You shall have no others gods before Me. You shall not make for yourself a graven image.

3. You shall not take the name of the Lord your God in vain.

4. Observe the Sabbath day and keep it holy.

5. Honor your father and your mother.

6. You shall not murder.

7. You shall not commit adultery.

8. You shall not steal.

9. You shall not bear false witness against your neighbor.

10. You shall not be jealous of your neighbor's wife, his house, his field, his man-or maid-servant, his ox, his donkey, or anything that is your neighbor's.

The Noahide Laws: Seven Commandments for all People

In Genesis 9 there are seven fundamental laws that are vital to the existence of human society. In ancient times, an Israelite was expected to carry out all of the commandments of the Five Books of Moses, whereas obedience to only these seven was required of non-Jews living among Israelites.

1. Not to believe in idolatry

2. Not to curse God

3. Not to commit murder

4. To have relations and a normal family life with only one wife

5. Not to commit thievery

6. Not to eat a piece of meat that is removed from its source while it is yet alive

7. To establish courts of justice to enforce the observance of the preceding six laws

Torah Portions from the Five Books of Moses Named after People

There are only six portions of the Torah that are named after a person:

1. *Balak*. The king of Moab, he hired Bilaam to curse the Jews.

2. *Chayyei Sarah*. The wife of Abraham and Judaism's first matriarch.

3. *Korach*. From the tribe of Levi, he and his followers were consumed by an earthquake.

4. *Noach*. A righteous person, who, along with his family, was saved from the flood.

5. *Pinchas*. The grandson of Aaron, the high priest.

6. *Yitro*. The father-in-law of Moses.

Translations of the Bible

The Hebrew Bible (called the "Old Testament" by Christians) has been translated into hundreds of different languages over the centuries. Here is a summary of some of the most important translations of the Bible:

1. **King James or Authorized Version of the Bible**. This Bible, commissioned by King James I of Great Britain, was completed in 1611. Until the present time it was considered the most historically accurate of all of the translations of the Bible.

2. **Latin Bible or Vulgate**. This authoritative Latin translation of the Bible was called the Vulgate, meaning "the language of the people." It was written in 404 c.e. by Jerome, the Bishop of Rome.

3. **New Version of the Holy Scriptures**. This Bible, created in the 1960s, is a revised edition of the 1917 Bible, produced under the auspices of the Jewish Publication Society of America.

4. **Samaritan Bible or Hexateuch**. This Bible, written in Hebrew, is a pre-Masoretic text. It is unusual in that it

contains six books—the Five Books of Moses and the Book of Joshua.

5. **Septuagint** (250 B.C.E.). This Bible, written in the second language into which the Bible was translated, Greek, was widely used by the Jews of the Byzantine Empire. The word *septuagint* means seventy, and this Bible was named after the seventy scholars who worked on its translation. The Septuagint is the accepted version of the Bible of the Greek church.

6. **Syriac Bible**. Sometimes called the *Peshitta*, meaning simple, this Bible is a literal translation from the Hebrew, written in the second century C.E.

7. **Targum of Jonathan**. (7th Cent. C.E.). This Aramaic translation bears the name of Jonathan ben Uzziel. It is more a paraphrase than a true translation and deals with the biblical portions related to the prophets. It was widely used in Babylon in the fourth century.

8. **Targum Onkelos**. (2nd Cent. C.E.). This Aramaic translation, used extensively by the Jews in Babylon, dates back to the beginning of the second century. It is believed that its translator, Onkelos, was a convert to Judaism.

9. **Targum Yerushalmi or Pseudo-Jonathan**. (7th Cent. C.E.). This Aramaic translation was used extensively by the Jews in Jerusalem in the seventh century.

10. **The 1854 Translation of the Bible**. This Bible was the work of Isaac Leeser, a well-known Philadephian rabbi. It remained an important translation for the Jews for fifty years.

11. **The 1917 Translation of the Bible**. This Bible was produced by a group of Jewish scholars under the auspices of the Jewish Publication Society of America.

12. **Tyndale's Bible**. (1531 C.E.). William Tyndale

translated his Bible into English directly from the Hebrew and the Greek. This translation was the first to be printed.

13. **Wycliffe Bible.** This was the first translation of the Christian Bible, containing the Hebrew Bible, the Apocrypha, and the New Testament, all of which were translated into English from the Latin. This Bible's translation has been attributed to John Wycliffe (1320–1384).

Transportation

The passages that follow describe some of the transportation methods used in biblical times.

MODES OF TRANSPORTATION

1. "Pharaoh said to Joseph, 'See, I have set you over all of Egypt.' . . . And he made him to ride in the second chariot which he had" (Genesis 41:41–43).

2. Joseph sent wagons to Canaan to carry back his father and his brothers' families (Genesis 45:17–21).

3. The Egyptians pursued the Israelites with the horses and chariots of Pharaoh (Exodus 14:9).

4. The Levites were given six covered wagons in which to carry the tabernacle and its furniture (Numbers 7:1–9).

5. The Philistines sent the ark of the covenant back to the Israelites on a cart pulled by a cow (I Samuel 6:7–14).

239

6. King Ahab rode into battle in a chariot but was killed by an Assyrian arrow (I Kings 22:34–38).

7. There appeared a chariot of fire, and horses of fire, and Elijah went up by a whirlwind into heaven (II Kings 2:11).

8. Jehu rode in a chariot and chased the chariots of King Ahaziah and King Joram, killing them both (II Kings 9:16–28).

9. Zechariah saw four chariots driven by angels (Zechariah 6:1–8).

LONGEST BIBLICAL JOURNEYS

1. Abraham moved his entire household from Haran to Canaan (Genesis 12:1–5).

2. The Israelites wandered through the desert for forty years after they had left Egypt to go to the Promised Land (Deuteronomy 29:5).

The Twelve Tribes of Israel

According to the Bible (Genesis 49), Jacob's twelve sons eventually became the twelve tribes of Israel. The following are the twelve tribes of Israel, their emblems, banners, and jewels:

Name	Emblem	Banner	Jewel
Asher	woman and olive tree	pearl color	beryl
Benjamin	wolf	multicolored	jasper
Dan	serpent	deep blue	jacinth
Ephraim	bullock	jet black	lapis lazuli
Gad	encampment	gray	crystal
Issachar	donkey	black; sun and moon	sapphire
Judah	lion	sky blue	turquoise
Levi	urim and thummim	white, red, black	emerald
Manasseh	unicorn	jet black	lapis lazuli
Naphtali	deer	wine color	amethyst
Reuben	mandrake	red	carnelian
Simeon	city of Shechem	green	topaz
Zebulun	ship	white	amethyst

Vocations

The vocations of the various characters are mentioned frequently throughout the Bible. The following is a partial listing of professions, with their references:

1. Apothecary (Nehemiah 3:8)
2. Archer (Genesis 21:20)
3. Astrologer (Daniel 1:20)
4. Baker (Genesis 40:1)
5. Barber (Ezekiel 5:1)
6. Binder of sheaves (Psalm 129:7)
7. Brickmaker (Exodus 5:7)
8. Builder (I Kings 5:18)
9. Butler (Genesis 40:1)
10. Camel driver (Genesis 32:13–16)
11. Candlestick maker (Exodus 25:31)

12. Chariot driver (I Kings 22:34)

13. Charmer (Psalm 58:5)

14. Cook (I Samuel 8:13)

15. Ditchdigger (Isaiah 22:11)

16. Diviner (I Samuel 6:2)

17. Embroiderer (Exodus 38:23)

18. Enchanter (Jeremiah 27:9)

19. Engraver (Exodus 38:23)

20. Forestkeeper (Nehemiah 2:8)

21. Furniture maker (Exodus 31:6–9)

22. Garment maker (Exodus 31:6)

23. Goatherder (Genesis 32:14)

24. Goldsmith (Isaiah 40:19)

25. Grape harvester (Jeremiah 6:9)

26. Harlot (Joshua 6:17)

27. Hewer of timber (II Chronicles 2:10)

28. Horseman (II Kings 9:17)

29. Hunter (Genesis 25:27)

30. Interpreter (Genesis 42:23)

31. Judge (II Samuel 15:4)

32. Lamp maker (Exodus 25:37)

33. Locksmith (Nehemiah 3:3)

34. Magician (Daniel 2:2)

35. Maidservant (Exodus 20:10)

36. Mariner (Ezekiel 27:27)

37. Mason (II Kings 12:12)

38. Midwife (Genesis 35:17)

39. Miner (Job 28:1–2)

40. Minstrel (II Kings 3:15)

41. Necromancer (Deuteronomy 18:11)

42. Night watchman (Isaiah 21:11)

43. Nurse (Exodus 2:7–9)

44. Planter (Jeremiah 31:15)

45. Postman (Esther 3:13)

46. Potter (Jeremiah 18:4)

47. Priest (Leviticus 1:7)

48. Prince (I Chronicles 5:6)

49. Prophet (I Samuel 3:20)

50. Queen (I Kings 10:1)

51. Refiner (Malachi 3:3)

52. Scientist (Daniel 1:4)

53. Servant (Genesis 2:2)

54. Sheepmaster (II Kings 3:4)

55. Shipbuilder (I Kings 22:48)

56. Singer (I Chronicles 9:33)

57. Snake charmer (Psalm 58:4)

58. Soothsayer (Joshua 13:22)

59. Spy (Joshua 2:1)

60. Stargazer (Isaiah 47:13)

61. Steward (Genesis 15:2)

62. Tailor (Exodus 39:22)

63. Treasurer (Ezra 1:8)

64. Watchman (II Kings 9:17)

65. Water drawer (Joshua 9:21)

66. Weaver (Exodus 35:35)

67. Witch (Exodus 22:18)

68. Wizard (Leviticus 20:27)

69. Woodcarver (Exodus 35:33)

70. Worker in brass (I Kings 7:13)

Wars and Battles

A multitude of battles and wars occurred during biblical times. The following is a partial list of the major battles and wars:

1. Abraham wages war against a Mesopotamian king to rescue his nephew Lot (Genesis 14:1–6).

2. Babylon attacks Judah (II Kings 25:1–3).

3. David defeats Goliath (I Samuel 17).

4. David defeats the Jebusites (II Samuel 5:6–9).

5. David defeats Moab (II Samuel 8:2).

6. Deborah defeats the northern Canaanites (Judges 4:1–16).

7. Egypt fights Jerusalem (I Kings 14:25–28).

8. Egypt defeats Josiah (II Kings 23:29–30).

9. Four lepers defeat the army of Syria (II Kings 16:24–25).

10. Gideon defeats the Midianites (Judges 7:9–25).

11. Israel defeats the Amalekites (Exodus 17:8–16).

12. Israel defeats the King of Bashan (Numbers 21:33–35).

13. Israel defeats Jabin, King of Hazor (Joshua 11:1–15).

14. Israel defeats Jericho (Joshua 6:1–27).

15. Israel defeats the Midianites (Numbers 31:6–12).

16. Israel defeats the Philistines (I Samuel 5:7–14).

17. Israel is victorious over Ai (Joshua 8:1–29).

18. Samson defeats the Philistines (Judges 15:9–15).

19. Saul defeats the Ammonites (I Samuel 11:1–11).

20. Uzziah defeats the Philistines (II Chronicles 26:6–7).

21. War of the Persian Jews against their enemies (Esther 9).

Water and Wells

Water is a most important commodity in any society. In ancient times the role of water was a vital one, and the importance of wells in the life of the community is often vividly portrayed in the Bible. The following are several important biblical wells:

1. *Bahurim.* Jonathan and Ahimaaz escaped Absalom's men by hiding in a well in Bahurim (II Samuel 17:17–21).

2. *Beeralahairoi.* The angel of God spoke to Hagar at the well called Beeralahairoi, situated between Kadesh and Bered (Genesis 16:7–14).

3. *Beersheba.* Avimelech's servants made a covenant at the well at Beersheba (Genesis 21:30).

4. *En Hakkore.* After Samson killed a thousand men using an ass's jawbone, he was very thirsty. God opened the ground and water poured forth. Samson called the well En Hakkore (Judges 15:19).

5. *Harod.* At the well of Harod God diminished Gideon's troops to the courageous three hundred (Judges 7:1–7).

6. *Midian.* Moses met his wife Zipporah when he helped her and her sisters water their flock at a well in the land of Midian (Exodus 2:15–21).

7. *Nahor.* Abraham's servant Eliezer found a wife for Isaac at the well near the city of Nahor (Genesis 24:11–20).

8. David longed to drink from the well at *Bethlehem.* Three men cut through the Philistine defenses and obtained water for him. David then poured the water out as a sacrifice for God (II Samuel 23:14–17).

9. Isaac's servants dug two wells that he gave up to other herdsmen instead of fighting over them. He called them *Esek* and *Sitnah.* They then dug two additional wells, called *Rehovot* and *Beersheba* (Genesis 26:17–33).

10. Jacob met Rachel when she came to water her sheep at a well that was covered by a stone (Genesis 29:1–12).

Weights and Measures

From the earliest period in their history, the Israelites were aware of the need for an accurate system of weights and measures. Leviticus 19:35–36 states, "You shall not falsify measures of length, weight, or capacity. You shall have an honest balance." The prophets, too, cautioned against the use of inaccurate measures. For instance, in Amos 8:5 we hear of greedy people saying, "If only the new moon were over, so that we could sell grain, the Sabbath, so that we could offer wheat for sale, using an *ephah* that is too small, and a shekel that is too big, tilting a dishonest scale, and selling refuse as grain."

An accepted system of weights for buying and selling, building, and measuring was based in biblical times on common physical phenomena such as the palm of the hand, the length of the arm, a day's journey, seeds of grain, and so forth. In biblical measurement, the custom was to distinguish between natural measures (i.e., those that refer to parts of the human anatomy) and more fixed measurements established by reckoning. Today it is very difficult to establish accurately the absolute values of the measures,

The Jewish Bible Almanac

because as early as the days of the Second Temple in Jerusalem the biblical measures were not precisely known. Any modern-day attempt to determine the exact amount of a biblical measurement is made on the basis of archaeological findings.

LINEAR MEASURE

Units of length are generally derived from the average measures of the length of human limbs. Interestingly enough, the names of measurements based on limbs are still often used today (e.g., foot).

In early biblical times, the custom was to measure the limbs themselves. For example, in Deuteronomy 3:11 the standard cubit was the part of the arm from the elbow to the tip of the middle finger, and the span was the distance between the tip of the little finger and the tip of the thumb with the fingers spread. A handbreadth was the width of four fingers, and a fingerbreadth was measured according to the width of the finger. Here is a cross section of biblical implements used for measuring small units of length.

1. **Measuring line**. "'See, a time is coming,' says God, 'when the city shall be rebuilt for God from the Tower of Chananel to the Corner Gate; and the measuring line shall go straight out to the Gareb Hill, and then toward Goah'" (Jeremiah 31:38).

2. **Measuring rod**. "In his hand were a cord of linen and a measuring rod" (Ezekiel 40:3).

3. **Rope**. "But this I swear, is what God said: 'Your wife shall play the harlot in the town, your sons and

daughters shall fall by the sword, and your land shall be divided up with rope'" (Amos 7:17).

4. **Thread**. "As for the columns, each was eighteen cubits high and the thread twelve cubits in circumference; it was hollow, and the metal was four fingers thick" (Jeremiah 52:21).

Five small units of length are mentioned in the Bible. Their exact length is not explicit, but their interrelations are generally established. The units are "reed," "cubit," "span," "handbreadth," and "fingerbreadth."

MEASUREMENTS OF BIBLICAL VOLUME

As was the case with linear measures, the human limbs were initially used to measure volume. Small units of volume included the handful (Leviticus 2:2), which is the measure of the grasp of three fingers, *chofen* (Exodus 9:8), which is the entire palm of the hand, and *chofnayin*, (Ecclesiastes 4:6) which is two handfuls. Agricultural receptacles for grain were also used as measures and included the *omer*, which was a bundle of ears of corn, and a "skin jar" (I Samuel 1:24), which held a certain quantity of wine. Here is a summary of ten biblical units of volume.

1. *Chomer*. "If anyone consecrates to the Lord any land that he holds, its assessment shall be in accordance with its seed requirement: fifty shekels of silver to a *chomer* of barley seed" (Leviticus 27:16).

2. *Ephah* "The *omer* is a tenth of an *ephah*" (Exodus 16:36).

3. *Hin.* "There shall be a tenth of a measure of choice flour with a quarter of a *hin* of beaten oil mixed in" (Exodus 29:40).

4. *Issaron.* "If, however, he is poor and his means are insufficient, he shall take one male lamb for a guilt offering, to be elevated in expiation for him, one-tenth *issaron* of choice flour with oil mixed in for a meal offering, and a *log* of oil" (Leviticus 14:21).

5. *Kav.* "There was a great famine in Samaria, and the seige continued until a donkey's head sold for eighty shekels of silver and a quarter of a *kav* of dove's dung" (I Kings 6:25).

6. *Kor* and *Bath.* "The due from the oil, the oil being measured by the *bath*, shall be one-tenth of a *bath* from every *kor*" (Ezekiel 45:14).

7. *Letech.* "Then I hired her for fifteen shekels of silver, a *chomer* of barley, a *letech* of barley . . ." (Hosea 3:2).

8. *Log.* "On the eighth day he shall take two male lambs without blemish, one ewe lamb in its first year without blemish, three-tenths of a measure of choice flour with oil mixed in for a meal offering, and one *log* of oil" (Leviticus 14:10).

9. *Omer.* "Gather as much of it as each of you requires to eat, an *omer* to a person for as many of you as there are" (Exodus 16:16).

10. *Se'ah.* "Abraham hastened to the tent of Sarah, and said, 'Quick, three *seahs* of choice flour!'" (Genesis 18:6).

The basic method of determining the values of these measures is to assess the volume of vessels, found in archaeological digs, that have the volume capacity marked on them. According to the calculations of W. F. Albright (1960), the royal bath had a capacity of 22 liters. Thus the scale of measures of volume based on this calculation would be as follows:

Chomer-kor	220 liters
Letech	110 liters
Ephah-bath	22 liters
Se'ah	7.3 liters
Hin	3.6 liters
Omer-issaron	2.2 liters
Kav	1.2 liters
Log	0.3 liters

BIBLICAL MEASURE OF AREA

The basic unit of biblical measurement of area was the *tzemed* (I Samuel 14:14), which refers to the area of land that a pair of oxen could plow in a single day's work. A second system of measuring area was based upon the quantity of seeds sown in it. For example, Leviticus 27:16 states, "If anyone consecrates to God any land that he holds, its assessment shall be in accordance with its seed requirement."

With regard to rectangular area, the Bible uses a more exact measurement system, usually noting the length and width of the rectangular area in cubits or parts of cubits and adding the word "square." For example, Exodus 27:1 states, "You shall make the altar of acacia wood, five cubits long and five cubits wide; the altar is to be a square and three cubits high."

BIBLICAL UNITS OF WEIGHT

The verb *shakal*, meaning "to weigh," is shared by all peoples of the Semitic languages. The majority of weights were made of stone; thus the Bible usually refers to weights as stones.

Seven major weights are mentioned in the Bible: talent, shekel, *beka*, *gerah*, *pim* and *kesitah*. The talent was the largest unit of biblical weight. The relationship between the talent and the shekel becomes apparent in verses 25–26 of Exodus 38:

> "The silver of those of the community who were recorded came to 100 talents and 1,775 shekels by sanctuary weight: a half-shekel a head, half a shekel by the sanctuary weight, for each one who was entered in the records, from the age of twenty years up, 603,550 men."

The half-shekel brought by 603,550 men amount to 100 talents and 1,775 shekels. Thus these calculations can be made between the shekel and the talent:

    603,500 half-shekels = 300,000 + 1,775 shekels
    300,000 shekels = 100 talents
    3,000 shekels = 1 talent

The shekel is the most basic weight, and its name in Hebrew actually means "weight." According to Exodus 30:13, the value of a *gerah* was one-twentieth part of a shekel. The *mina* (Ezekiel 45:12) designates a weight of approximately fifty to sixty shekels.

The *beka*, mentioned in Genesis 24:22 and Exodus 38:26, has been determined to be one-half a shekel.

If one measures a **mina** as fifty shekels, the following table may be established:

	talent	*mina*	shekel	*beka*	*gerah*
talent	1				
mina	60	1			
shekel	3,000	50	1		
beka	6,000	100	2	1	
gerah	60,000	1000	20	10	1

Also mentioned in the Bible is the *peres* (Daniel 5:25, 28). Some biblical scholars have suggested that the **peres** is the equivalent of half a **mina**.

UNITS OF TIME

The following are some of the units of time mentioned in the Bible:

1. **Chodesh:** A period of one month (Lev. 25:22).

2. **Jubilee** (Leviticus 25:9–22). refers to the fiftieth year. The Bible ordained a rest from agricultural work in ancient Israel once every seven years. Any crops grown in the seventh year became communal property. The year following seven fallow years, that is, the fiftieth year, was called the Jubilee Year. (*shnat ha'yovel* in Hebrew) At this time, cultivation was prohibited, slaves were freed, and land purchases since the previous Jubilee reverted to their original owners.

3. **Shabbat:** The seventh day of the week (known as the Sabbath), a blessed day of rest (Exodus 20:8, 9, 10).

4. *Shana*: A period of one year (Exodus 12:2).

5. *Shemitta*, or Sabbatical Year: The Bible ordained a rest from agricultural work in Israel once every seven years (Leviticus 25:3–7). Any crops grown in the seventh year were to become communal property, and slaves were allowed to go free.

The Wicked and their Punishments

There are many references to the wicked in the Bible. The following are ten biblical signs of the wicked:

1. They borrow and do not pay back (Psalm 37:21).

2. They plot (Psalm 37:12).

3. They walk on every side (Psalm 12:8).

4. They oppress (Psalm 17:9).

5. They boast (Psalm 10:3).

6. They are estranged from the womb (Psalm 58:3).

7. They are filled with mischief (Proverbs 12:21).

8. They have drawn out the sword (Psalm 37:14).

9. They lay snares (Psalm 119:110).

10. They have hearts like postsherds (Proverbs 26:23).

PUNISHMENTS FOR THE WICKED

The Bible has its share of punishments for people who have been deemed wicked. The following are ten punishments for wicked people listed in the Bible:

1. The wicked shall be burnt up in flames (Psalm 106:18).

2. The wicked shall fall in their own nets (Psalm 14:10).

3. The wicked shall be ashamed (Psalm 31:17).

4. The wicked shall be shaken (Job 38:13).

5. The wicked shall be silent (I Samuel 2:9).

6. The wicked shall be condemned (Deuteronomy 25:1).

7. The wicked shall be turned into hell (Psalm 9:17).

8. The wicked shall not inhabit the earth (Proverbs 10:30).

9. The wicked shall perish (Psalm 37:20).

10. The wicked shall drink the dregs of the wine (Psalm 75:8).

Who's Who in the Bible

The following is an alphabetical list of important personalities in the Torah, The Five Books of Moses:

Aaron. Elder brother of Moses

Abel. Second son of Adam and Eve

Abraham. First patriarch and founder of Hebrew nation

Adam and **Eve.** First man and woman in the Bible

Balaam. Heathen prophet whose intended curse of the Israelites turned into a blessing

Balak. King of Moab

Benjamin. Youngest son of Jacob

Cain. Eldest son of Adam and Eve

Caleb. Leader of tribe of Judah

Dan. Fifth son of Jacob

Dinah. Daughter of Jacob and Leah

Enoch. Eldest son of Cain

Ephraim. Youngest son of Joseph

Esau. Son of Isaac and elder twin brother of Jacob

Gad. Seventh son of Jacob

Gershon. Eldest of Levi's three sons

Hagar. Mother of Ishmael and Egyptian handmaid of Sarah

Ham. Son of Noah

Haran. Brother of Abraham

Heth. Son of Canaan

Isaac. Second of the three patriarchs

Ishmael. Eldest son of Abraham

Israel. New name given to Jacob

Issachar. Fifth son of Jacob and Leah

Jacob. Third of the patriarchs

Japheth. Son of Noah

Jethro. Midianite priest and father of Zipporah

Joseph. Son of Jacob and Rachel

Judah. Fourth son of Jacob's first wife, Leah

Keturah. Abraham's second wife

Korah. Levite, related to Moses, who rebelled against Moses and Aaron

Laban. Brother of Rebekah

Lamech. Father of Noah

Leah. Daughter of Laban and wife of Jacob

Levi. Third son of Jacob and Leah

Lot. Son of Abraham's brother Haran

Manasseh. First son of Joseph and Asenath

Melchizedek. King of Salem

Methusaleh. Son of Enoch and oldest person recorded in the Bible

Miriam. Elder sister of Moses

Moses. Prophet and founder of Jewish people

Nahshon. Chief of tribe of Judah

Naphtali. Sixth son of Jacob

Noah. Hero of the flood narratives.

Onan. Son of Judah

Pharaoh. Permanent title of king of Egypt in ancient times

Phineas. Priest and grandson of Aaron

Potiphar. Chief of Pharaoh's bodyguard

Puah. One of midwives who disobeyed Pharaoh's orders to kill the Hebrew male children at birth

Rachel. Second wife of Jacob

Rebekah. Wife of Isaac and mother of Jacob and Esau

Reuben. Eldest son of Jacob and Leah

Sarah. Wife of Abraham and mother of Isaac

Shem. Son of Noah

Simeon. Second son of Jacob

Tamar. Wife of Er

Terah. Father of Abraham

Zebulun. Sixth son of Jacob and Leah

Zelophehad. Israelite of the tribe of Manasseh whose five daughters claimed the right, until then reserved to sons, to inherit their father's land

Zipporah. Wife of Moses

For Further Reading

Albright, William Foxwell. *The Archaeology of Palestine.* Harmondsworth: Penguin Books, 1949.

Babylonian Talmud. Tractate Ta'anit. London: Soncino Press, 1960.

Comay, Joan. *Who's Who in the Old Testament.* Pillar Books, 1971.

Eisenberg, Azriel. *The Book of Books.* London: Soncino Press, 1976.

Ewert, David. *From Ancient Tablets to Modern Translations.* Michigan: Zondervan Publishing House, 1983.

Margolis, Max L. *Hebrew Scriptures in the Making.* Philadelphia: Jewish Publication Society, 1948.

Olitzky, Kerry M. and Isaacs, Ronald H. *The Second How To Handbook for Jewish Living.* New Jersey, Ktav, 1996.

Sivan, Gabriel. *The Bible and Civilization.* Jerusalem: Keter Publishing House, 1973.

Wollman-Tsamir, Pinchas. *The Graphic History of the Jewish Heritage.* New York: Shengold, 1963.

Index

About the Author

Rabbi Ronald Isaacs is the rabbi of Temple Sholom in Bridge-water, New Jersey. He received his doctorate in instructional technology from Columbia University's Teacher's College. He is the author of numerous books, including *Words for the Soul: Jewish Wisdom for Life's Journey, Mitzvot, A Sourcebook for the 613 Commandments*, and *Close Encounters: Jewish Views about God*. Rabbi Isaacs currently serves on the Board of *Shofar* Magazine, the Rabbinical Assembly, and C.A.J.E. He resides in New Jersey with his wife, Leora, and their children Keren and Zachary.